T0356935

Who Is the
Real Hog?

Robert Scot Michel

authorHOUSE®

AuthorHouse™
1663 Liberty Drive
Bloomington, IN 47403
www.authorhouse.com
Phone: 1-800-839-8640

Published by AuthorHouse 6/24/2013

ISBN: 978-1-4817-5946-5 (sc)
ISBN: 978-1-4817-5947-2 (e)

Library of Congress Control Number: 2013909926

This book is dedicated to Robert Jerrahian, Herman Garbisch, and Davey Warren, district sales managers for Harley-Davidson Motor Company. Each was a mentor to me and passed away too soon while an employee of the Motor Company.

TABLE OF CONTENTS

INTRODUCTION

WHY ARE SO MANY people dedicated to Harley-Davidson? I am amazed that everywhere I go, around the world, I see people wearing Harley-Davidson T-shirts. Some of the T-shirts have the Harley logo on the front and a statement on the back, such as, "On the eighth day, God created Harley" or "God rides a Harley." These people don't mean to be sacrilegious, they are just expressing their passion and belief in a product that they are in love with forever. What makes people put a tattoo on their body with the trademark of the company that produces a product they own? Some people even name their children and pets after this product. I think the word that best describes how enthusiasts feel about Harley-Davidson is *passion*.

Most people don't know the recent history of the Motor Company. I became an employee in 1984. Prior to that, Harley-Davidson was owned by AMF, a company best known in the sporting-goods industry, especially for bowling. It was a very large corporation and, in the grand scheme of things, served Harley-Davidson very well. Harley got a manufacturing plant in York, Pennsylvania, and a new engine-manufacturing facility in Milwaukee, Wisconsin. In the late '60s, Harley-Davidson was nearly broke, and the company was looking for buyers of all its assets. Rodney Gott from AMF arranged a friendly buyout of Harley-Davidson. Many years later, Harley-Davidson would name the museum in York, Pennsylvania, after him.

In 1981, AMF decided profits from Harley were not good enough and tried to sell the company regardless of the results. Quality of the product had gone down, and competition from the Japanese had increased intensely. The only company interested in buying was Bangor Punta, and it was going to buy Harley-Davidson for pennies on the dollar. Vaughn Beals, the president of Harley-Davidson at the time but an employee of AMF, gathered together a group of executives and purchased the company from AMF. The financier was Citicorp. At the time, the economy was bad, Harley-Davidson had mandated many layoffs, the remaining employees had to take pay cuts, and the company was forced to do more with less. Even under these circumstances, the vast majority of employees decided to stay with the company. *Passion*.

Under the direction of Vaughn Beals, the company saw many improvements and small increases in profits. He instituted just-in-time inventory, strategic statistical analysis, the evolution engine, and many more improvements. Despite these changes and for reasons unknown, by late 1984 Citicorp decided to stop financing its investment in Harley-Davidson. From my perspective, Citicorp decided that its return on investment was not good enough to continue the relationship.

What happened? How did Harley-Davidson get into this position? I think it was corporate greed on Citicorp's part. Let me tell you more about how these executives saved the company. Harley had been paying Citicorp very high interest rates. Our retail customers were pay up to 29 percent interest on their motorcycles, and I think Harley was paying about 20 percent on its loan to Citicorp. And even though it was making a profit, Citicorp probably thought that it could use its money in a better way in other investments. Unfortunately for Harley, when they went looking for other financing, the question always came up about Citicorp no longer wanting to be involved.

A year later, Harley-Davidson was at the end of its rope. Rich Teerlink, the company's CFO, had been searching for financing all year long. Citicorp had made it clear that there would be no January 1, 1986. It was calling the loan and closing the credit lines. A few months earlier, Rich had established a deal with a financial institution out of Chicago. But near Christmas of 1985, the deal began to go sour. If not for a dedicated Harley-Davidson rider at that company, the deal would have never happened.

On December 31, 1985, Rich Teerlink was waiting anxiously for the loan approval. He convinced many banks that were involved to keep key people at work until the deal was closed. At 11:46 p.m., all the funds had been transferred into a Wisconsin bank, and the company survived by a mere fourteen minutes. Profits began to grow, and in 1986 the board of directors listed Harley-Davidson on the American Stock Exchange, selling its stock publicly. At that time, I was incredibly excited, but I have since learned how the evils of corporate greed can have a detrimental influence on any company and its employees (and their families), which filters down into the entire local community.

I say that the company was saved by the passion of the customers, employees, and dealers. During the bad economic times that have most recently afflicted us all, the new Harley management regime has opted for more layoffs and facility closures. This may be under the guise of the efficiency.

But remember, there is always competition and the economy to deal with ... at all times. Can and will Harley-Davidson compete? Even if the answer is yes, will corporate greed hinder or harm this company again? If you destroy the passion in your people, you destroy the entire infrastructure, and your house of cards may start to tumble down.

CHAPTER 1

TO HARLEY OR NOT TO HARLEY

IT WAS A BEAUTIFUL warm spring day in San Diego. I decided to go for a jog and drove my rental car over the bridge to Coronado Island. I made my way to the beach and parked in front of the house featured in the movie *Top Gun*. I got out of the car, did a little stretching, and started my run heading north toward the air-force base. The F-14 navy pilots were practicing touch-and-go landings on the airstrip up ahead. It was pretty cool watching the jets glide in silently and touch down, and then hear the deafening roar of the massive engines as the jets took off again.

Whenever I go for a short run, it provides a perfect time for some peaceful thinking. My longer runs start out with a lot of thinking and turn into more of a Zen-like exercise. This was going to be a short thirty- to forty-five-minute run. I started thinking about the past week's events. I had already been in San Diego visiting my best buddy, Jim, for about two weeks. In the past week, Jim had arranged for me to meet his boss at Wausau Insurance Company to discuss a job opening as a sales agent for

Southern California based out of San Diego office. Jim had worked for Wausau for about five years, starting as an underwriter in our hometown of Milwaukee. Jim got married, moved to San Diego, got divorced, and was living a bachelor's dream in California. Anyway, I went into the interview without any expectations, as I lived in Milwaukee and wasn't looking to relocate. I really just wanted to see what his boss and Wausau had to offer. I had a great interview and within the hour was offered the job. I would start as a trainee selling business insurance with a great base salary and a handsome commission schedule. It all happened so fast that I told the guy that I needed several days to think about the offer.

The day after that interview, my brother Eddie (who was in charge of the test riders at Harley) called me from Milwaukee and told me that there was a job opening for a district manager trainee at Harley-Davidson. He said that if I was interested, I needed to get my résumé to him as soon as possible. As I was running, I kept thinking about the potential of each position. I mean, insurance sales is not easy, but if you stick to it, after a while your book of business grows and your commissions continue to greatly increase. And I would be living in Southern California with my buddy Jim. I kept picturing myself living in a cool condo, driving a convertible Porsche, enjoying the gorgeous weather year round, and living the bachelor's dream. Meanwhile, everything in the news about Harley-Davidson was pretty negative. The company's future looked bleak. It was early 1984, when most Harley riders were thought of by the common man as members of the Hells Angels. Honda had tried its best with its marketing slogan, "You meet the nicest people on a Honda." They had also done an excellent job with the quality and reliability of their motorcycles. Nevertheless, motorcycling in general and Harley-Davidson in particular had a bad reputation. Harley-Davidsons also had very poor performance and horrible reliability. But if you were a man's man, Harley-Davidson still was the coolest motorcycle ever made. I spent a few hours on the phone with my brother discussing my concerns about the future of the company. He had just returned from participating in the Cannonball One Lap of America, an event sponsored by screenwriter and automotive columnist Brock Yates. Harley-Davidson had entered the race with an FXRT Sport Glide. It had the new Evolution engine that Harley was planning on putting in all its motorcycles.

The Cannonball One Lap was an 8,704-mile endurance run around America's perimeter, which had to be covered in just seven days of around-the-clock driving. The start and finish line was Darien, Connecticut, with official checkpoints in Ann Arbor, Michigan; Tumwater, Washington; Redondo Beach, California; and Jacksonville, Florida. Drivers were given route instructions for the next part of the course at each checkpoint. The objective was to cross the finish line exactly seven driving days (168 hours, to the second) after the departure, requiring vehicle and crew to be on the road twenty-four hours a day. A mandatory twenty-four-hour layover in Redondo Beach was not on the clock. Harley-Davidson had the only motorcycle entry in the field of approximately eighty vehicles. The company decided to enter one week prior to the April 13 start date, and it had no choice but to pull a brand-new motorcycle off the assembly line and go for it. The whole idea to participate was the brainchild of my friend Hal, who at that time was a district sales manager for Harley up in the Northeast.

Team Harley-Davidson, as it was called, consisted of district manager Hal, Talladega test mechanic Rick Jones, Gerry Knackert, and my brother, engineering test coordinator Eddie Michel. They all took shifts riding the motorcycle, then driving, sleeping, or navigating in the support van. Their efforts were supported at the front end with a sophisticated computer routing program developed by Harley-Davidson engineers, providing time to location routing coordinates. Without the proper benefits of routine break-in or regularly scheduled maintenance procedures, the motorcycle went the entire 8,704-mile distance without problems. Only one oil change was performed, in Redondo Beach (which is also where one of the support staff was buying drugs out of the back of the van during a news conference). My brother Eddie informed me that they never needed to change a tire or adjust the chain. They used about 150 gallons of gas and attained nearly sixty miles per gallon. They averaged approximately fifty-two mph day and night, including gas stops. One of the riders did get busted by the other three, as he was getting so tired on one of his riding shifts that he pulled out the choke knob to run the bike out of gas sooner and end his shift early. I guess I can see that happening, as it was a grueling around-the-clock run.

As one of the riders of the motorcycle around America, my brother assured me of the mechanical reliability of the new engine and that this would be the first stepping-stone in the successful future of the company. What was my decision?

Suddenly, something interrupted my train of thought. As I had been jogging and thinking, I had also been watching the jets come and go. But this time something was very different—the same jet had flown by several times without touching down. The pilot would bring that jet very close to the ground and then hit the throttle and take the jet back up in the air. Then I noticed that the hook used to stop the jet on an aircraft carrier had been deployed. It was just hanging out, and I am sure it would have caused serious problems if the pilot had tried to land on the runway. The air-force fire trucks were screaming up and down each side of the runway. By now I was at the end of that public beach at the security fence by the air-force base. So I was only a couple hundred yards away, and I got that nervous feeling in my stomach as I realized that some young pilot in training had to deal with a potential deadly situation. I stopped and stretched for a while and then turned around and headed back toward my car. I later found out from Jim's brother Dave, who was a naval aviator, that everything turned out okay.

As I was driving back to the house through downtown San Diego, I decided I would fly back to Milwaukee and go to an interview at Harley-Davidson. Jim and I spent the weekend partying downtown, and I flew home on a Monday. In the meantime, my brother had arranged an interview for me with a guy by the name of Clyde Fessler.

My brother told me not to bother dressing up for the interview and that most everyone at the company wore

Harley T-shirts. I just couldn't do that, so I wore casual sport-coat-and-tie-type outfit. I went to the security shack at the corner of 37th and Juneau Avenue. As I was checking in by giving them my name, the guards asked me if I was Eddie Michel's brother. I said yes, and they told me to go right in and that I would find Clyde's office down the hall on the left. When I opened the doors, I was amazed at what a dump this place was. Now understand, I was in the parts-and-accessories building and not the main office building. The parts-and-accessories building also held the entire warehouse for all of Harley-Davidson. The office area that I was overlooking appeared to be something out of the 1930s or 1940s. I made my way to Clyde's office and knocked on the door. After a few seconds, just as I was about to knock again, a gruff voice shouted, "Come in." Now this was cool: the overhead lights were turned off and two desk lamps lit the office. The office was completely filled with everything that had anything to do with Harley-Davidson motorcycles. Whole gas tanks, half gas tanks, handlebars, stickers, emblems, helmets, leather jackets, trophies, posters, and photos. It really was *so cool!* Clyde was on his phone with his back to me and his feet up on the credenza; he turned slightly and motioned for me to sit down. He got off the phone, and we talked a little about my history in sales and why I like motorcycling and what type of motorcycle I had (a Triumph) and why I might want to work at Harley.

After talking about that for five minutes, Clyde got another phone call. He turned his back again, put his feet up on the credenza, and talked for about fifteen minutes. He must have forgotten that I was in the room, because all of a sudden he told the other party, "Hang on," and then he pressed the telephone to his chest. He made this statement: "So, you are Eddie Michel's brother, right?" Then he asked me what I was doing for the weekend, and I told him that I was going on a motorcycle ride with my friend to the Mississippi River. Nearly before I got the words "Mississippi River" out of my mouth, he said, "You're hired! See Sheryl in Human Resources across the street."

CHAPTER 2

THIS IS IT?

MY FIRST POSITION AT Harley-Davidson was parts-and-accessories representative for all the Harley dealers in the eastern half of the United States. It actually was a pretty simple job. Essentially I took orders for replacement parts and accessories from my dealers and coordinated their timely delivery. The dealers and their parts managers were great people to talk with. The toughest and worst part of the job was dealing with back orders. As you can imagine, people get pretty angry when they have to wait days or weeks or months for parts to make their vehicle operational. I got pretty good at creating resources around the organization for getting my hands on those back-ordered parts even though I was not working within normal channels. Back in the early '80s, the entire warehouse was located at 3700 W. Juneau Avenue. Cory, the warehouse manager, knew my brother very well and would always help me if he could. Some of the guys in engineering and at York, Pennsylvania, also knew my brother and would help me if they could.

It was exciting to meet all the new people I was going to work with. It was an interesting mix of people. One of our team's boss guys was a big and tall, blond-haired, blue-eyed, fat Baby Huey–looking asshole. He was arrogant and condescending. He was also an ass-kisser. He would be at work before anyone got there and stay until everyone left at night, except he would be reading a newspaper. He really wanted to become a district manager. And it seemed like everything he did was planned to make him look good to his boss. But my coworkers were pretty cool—Teri, Carol, Marti, Chucky, Scott, and David. I did have to suffer through the initial time of getting to know everyone. Scott was hired on the same day I was, and he was in charge of parts and accessories for the western half of the United States. He was a real go-getter. Chucky looked like he was fifteen years old. Carol was so kind, wonderful, and experienced, and so was Marti, who would later become one of my best friends. My feeling was David was a henpecked guy who had a trophy business on the side. In the cubicle next to mine were a district manager and his secretary. His name was Chuck Russell and her name was Leah. They were really cool! I was really happy that my desk was so close to Chuck because, as a district manager, he gave me invaluable advice. He wasn't from the South but had a little bit of a Southern country-boy way of talking. He had a dry sense of humor and was always joking. As the first six months of my employment wore on, he and my brother Eddie were really the only reasons that I stayed at Harley.

It wasn't too long after I started that the arrogant Baby Huey took one of the motorcycles from the company-owned vehicle pool for a weekend ride. On Monday morning he was a little banged up, and he told everyone that a deer had jumped in front of him and he lost control. He said the bike was okay but then he ran out of gas in the middle of the ghetto. He went to make a phone call and when he got back the motorcycle had been stolen. Yeah, right! My coworkers and I think what really happened was that he was driving through the city, lost control because he was not a good motorcycle rider, and was so embarrassed that he just left the keys in the motorcycle and ran away. He was the first one to get promoted to district manager. His territory was the state of Illinois. After the first week he was gone, his replacement found a lot of important work that was time-sensitive hidden in the bottom of his desk drawer. Sales management flew to Illinois and fired him after his first week. Just as he deserved.

Clyde, the guy who hired me, had created a club a couple years earlier called the Harley Owners Group, or HOG for short. One of my first traveling assignments was to Massillon, Ohio, to work at the Ohio state HOG event. Nobody really told me what to expect, and I was just going there as a body to be used for any type of work that was required. It turned out that the weather was beautiful and I finally got to meet thousands of our customers in one place. There's not a lot to do in Massillon, but it was great! I got to meet a district manager legend, Davey Warren, and a Harley legend, Willie G. Davidson. We had some displays and a few vendors who sold trinkets and trash from their ten-by-ten-foot booths. Harley-Davidson corporate also sponsored test rides with the entire selection of our new models, including the new Evolution engine. One of my coworkers, Clint, worked the event with me. The first night in the hotel room, he asked me if I wanted to smoke some stuff with him and I graciously declined. I hadn't smoked as much as a cig since I was seventeen years old. (Clint went on to be a long-term employee and became a hero. He witnessed a drunk driver killing a Wisconsin State Trooper and, with courage and the values of a simple Midwesterner, followed him and led the authorities to the man.) Later that night, one of the female customers who I had met during the day and had a great conversation with knocked on my motel-room door and wanted to know if we could just have meaningless sex! I enthusiastically agreed to her request.

I realized after that trip that if you were halfway decent looking and had a Harley-Davidson business card, there would be a bunch of groupies you could take your pick from if you wanted to. Except for the time I was married, I took full advantage of that fact. Women when I wanted them, and none with the last name Michel.

Nearly all of the employees were required to attend and work our annual national dealer show. It happened every year in July, when Harley corporate would introduce the new models for the upcoming year. If you know your history, Harley-Davidson was experiencing very difficult market conditions as well as economic battles at that time. About 25 percent of the dealers had formed a group called the Dealer Alliance Group. At that time, the president of the group was from Black River Falls, Wisconsin. They really had no power, and they were kind of like a thorn in the side of the corporation. In an effort to defuse the mob, Harley decided to hold two different dealer shows in two different locations. In 1984, there was a dealer show in Hump, Nevada, and one in Nashville, Tennessee. I was asked to attend the dealer show in Nashville, which just happened to be on the same weekend as my ten-year high-school reunion. One of the upper sales managers was Pat. I had discussed leaving early from the dealer show to attend my reunion and he agreed. But when I reminded him right before I left, he told me there was no way. That really pissed me off. I had been warned very early on about what a sneaky little shit he was. One of the district managers from the Ohio area, Harry, had gone to my high school many years earlier with my sister Gini. When I was telling him about the situation, he told me to just go ahead and leave when I needed to, and Pat probably would never even know about it. And if he ever found out, I should confront him and tell him that he had promised me that I could go to my reunion. That's exactly what I did.

The show was quite uneventful except for getting to meet Vaughn Beals, the president of the Motor Company. He was an amazing man, both in his personal presence as well as his personality. I was truly impressed. Every new model announcement meeting concludes with a beautiful dinner called the president's dinner. That night I met some girl whose brothers owned the dealership in western New York. We ended up going back to my room and making out for a couple hours. She really wanted to have sex, but I thought that I might get in trouble getting involved with one of our customers or dealers.

The very next month, I was required to go on a district-manager training and traveling week with a district manager, and as it turned out, it happened to be Harry from Ohio. This was pretty cool. I was actually going to go out and travel with the district manager for a week and find out what he did every single day at the dealerships as well as the paperwork and communications that he was responsible for. Harry lived in Brownstown, Ohio, so that's where we started. We visited dealers in western Pennsylvania and Ohio. One of the dealers near Cleveland took us out after work for drinks, and in this tiny little bar we ran into the investigative reporter Geraldo Rivera! Ha, one of my first celebrities, and he was there with his bodyguards, probably because he was only about five-foot-three. Another dealer from the Cleveland area invited us to dinner at his home. He had a sprawling estate on the river, and down the hill from the house was a big hot tub. His girlfriend gave us dinner and we headed to the hot tub. It was a beautiful Midwestern summer night, and his girlfriend walked up and down that hill bringing us beer all night long. I woke up with one of the worst hangovers I've ever had.

In the middle of the next day Harry got a phone call from his boss, David, telling him to head over immediately to a dealership that had just been discovered to be having serious financial problems. Coincidentally, it also happened to be the dealership owned by David's father. Every corporation, like the federal government, has its own checks and balances. Harley-Davidson used the company ITT Financial Resources as the financial arm for the dealers to purchase their motorcycles. Just like an automobile dealership, the vast majority of the inventory of vehicles that the dealership has are owned by either the manufacturer or a financial institution. In some ways, they are the guardian of all the merchandise that the dealership has on credit. Well, ITT Financial had discovered that this dealer had sold several motorcycles many weeks earlier and had not paid what was due. Harry and a representative from ITT Financial were ordered to get to the dealership and together insist upon immediate payment or proof that the vehicles were still in the dealer's possession. If a dealer cannot produce either the money or the evidence of the vehicle's state, then under federal law, the guarantor—in this case either Harley-Davidson or ITT Financial—is allowed to take possession of all assets of the small company to satisfy the obligation. This particular agreement is called the UCC Filing. It stands for Universal Commercial Code. Basically, when small-business owners have a line of credit, they have signed an obligation to ensure that when they sell an item owned by that creditor, they will pay immediately for the merchandise they just sold.

I arrived in Akron, Ohio, at this little craphole of a shop and met this good-looking and smooth-talking Southern boy from Texas who was the representative from ITT Financial. He had a full cast on his left leg, as he had recently been in motorcycle accident. Harry and this guy met in the parking lot and planned their strategy. They went in together and demanded either the motorcycles or the money, and when David's father, Mr. Smith could not produce either one, they both went to make phone calls. Now I was going to be involved in something that we called "scooping." Essentially, you immediately contact law enforcement and attorneys and begin to execute your right to repossess anything in the building—including the building—that will help fulfill the lack of payment. Essentially, you are taking everything this person has ever worked for to satisfy his debt to you. As I would later find out, this is a very emotional experience for both the business owner and those doing the repossession or scoop. As Mr. Smith continued to swear and lie and try to get out of the situation, the representative from ITT Financial finally told him to step outside, and said that if he was twenty years younger and if he personally did not have the cast on he would kick Mr. Smiths ass! I flew home the next day. When I returned to work on Monday, I wrote a thank-you letter to every dealer I'd met—except for David's father, of course.

One night in late December, I had volunteered to entertain a new dealer and his wife from Illinois. Ralph was a pretty cool guy, and he had a beautiful wife. He had recently sold his Snap-on franchise and purchased a small and struggling Harley dealership far outside of the Chicago area. After a full day of training, I took them out to dinner at one of Milwaukee's famous German restaurants, Mader's. After dinner, we went back to the Pfister Hotel and had drinks in the Bombay Bicycle Club. We were talking all about Harley business when some guy in the bar overheard us and staggered over to talk at us. He was a big fat guy dressed in a nice suit and had a full drink in his hand, not that he needed any more, and he proceeded to identify himself as one of the vice presidents of Citicorp bank. In his drunkenness, he started telling us what a mistake these new dealers had made because he was there on orders of his superiors to call the loan on Harley-Davidson and shut the company down. In as polite fashion as possible, I escorted him away from the new dealers and went back to them, explaining that he was just some drunk and not to even worry about anything he said. Little did I know, but it was true. I wrote about that in my introduction.

One of my absolute favorite memories is walking down the hallway at the corporate headquarters on Juneau Avenue and running into Willie G. He worked with his top designer, Louie Netz, who was also best friends with my brother Eddie. So Willie G. would often call me by my nickname, Bowzer! Walking down the hall after lunch one day, Willie was just coming back from what I suspected to be a liquid lunch. He saw me in the hallway and yelled as loud as he could, "Hey Bowzer! Remember, Harley's best, fuck the rest!"

As winter approached, the search for hiring ten new district managers was in full swing. I knew I had been favored because of my brother Eddie as well as how I had done my job and the unique experiences I'd had during my training. Out of all the applicants, of whom there were hundreds, Marti was given the first opportunity to pick the territory that he wanted. He chose North and Texas. I was given the second choice. I had been thinking about this a lot and wanted to stay close to home, so I chose Indiana. After I made my decision, I was invited into the VP's office, where Jim Patterson told me that Indiana would not work, and why.

Every organization should have an advisory group. You know, a board of directors for someone or some people who can help advise them. Harley-Davidson did have a board of directors, and it also had a customer group that was made up of dealers with elected officials called the Dealer Advisory Council. In 1984, the president of the Dealer Advisory Council was Howard, and he was the dealer near Washington, DC. Somehow during my short tenure, Howard had found out about me and requested that I be his district manager. During this meeting, Jim Patterson made it very clear that I had no choice—that was going to be my territory. He told me to buy a boat instead of a house and dock it and live on it in the Chesapeake Bay.

Over our Christmas shutdown, which was typically ten to twelve days, I traveled to Washington, DC, and started looking for homes to buy or rent. Even with my substantial base-pay raise, there was no way I could afford anything in that area. I came back to Milwaukee disappointed and went to pick up my new company car from the Harley-Davidson dealer, who also had a car dealership in Thiensville, Wisconsin. Wayne personally presented the car to me and congratulated me and wished me good luck. Wayne and his family later bought a Harley dealership, and we have been friends ever since that time. So off I went in my navy blue 1984 Chrysler LeBaron to Washington, DC, to start my job as a district sales manager for Harley-Davidson Motor Company. I lived in hotels, tried to learn my job, and looked for a place to live for the next six months.

CHAPTER 3

THIS IS HARDER THAN I THOUGHT . . .

BOB JERRAHIAN WAS A current district manager for my new territory, and I spent the next week or two traveling with him, meeting the new dealers, and getting to know the territory from his perspective. Bob was a cool guy. He had worked for the Motor Company for many, many years as a district manager and knew the territory and the dealers well. I began my training with the philosophy that I should just keep my mouth shut and listen, and only ask questions when I didn't understand. I got that advice from my brother's friend Hal. The first company meeting we had as district managers was held in Milwaukee at the Hilton Hotel downtown. It was a weeklong meeting, eight in the morning till five o'clock at night, followed by eating and drinking and partying and talking until the bar closed. I got to meet all the new district managers as well as all the existing district managers and a virtual parade of every manager from Harley corporate who had anything to do with the dealer network. That was a long week! When it was all over on Friday late afternoon, I went to the bar to have a drink. I was sitting by myself trying to stop my head from swimming from all the information that had just been pounded into me.

Hal walked into the bar, recognized me, and immediately came over and pulled up a bar stool and lit up a cigarette. He could tell by the look of consternation on my face that I was overwhelmed and said, "So boy … what you think of all that bullshit?" He was looking at the two-foot pile of manuals, policies, and procedures that we had received during our training week.

I asked him, "Out of all this stuff, what's the most important?"

The next thing that happened I will remember for the rest of my life as if it were yesterday. He yelled out, "Hey, barkeep! Come over here. Bring me some bar whiskey and a napkin!" All of a sudden, everything seemed like a scene out of a movie. In slow motion, the bartender filled a glass with ice and poured in the whiskey. He had a bar towel draped over his left arm when he brought the drink and a napkin. Hal took a big drag off his cigarette, exhaled, and took a big guzzle of his drink. He put the cigarette back in his mouth and cocked his head so that the smoke would not get into his eyes. He pulled out a pen, grabbed the napkin, and as he started to write, he said, "Here you go, boy." He spoke out loud as he wrote, saying, "Rule number one: Don't cheat and turn in all your expense reports. Rule number two …" and he stopped and thought, taking a large drag off his cigarette again, and said, "There are no other rules!" He put the pen down and pushed the napkin over to me, finished his drink, and left the bar. I think I was starting to understand. Times were desperate!

I was really starting to love Washington, DC, with all of its history and the monuments and the cool places to go. I tracked down an old high-school friend of mine, Belinda, and her husband, Mark, who were now living in Alexandria but in the process of moving into the city. It really was great to have familiar and friendly faces around me, being so far away from home. We often met at this cool bar called the Brick Street Saloon right in the middle of downtown DC. We usually met there along with many of their friends and made our way walking to other bars as the night went on. I was actually getting pretty good at navigating my way around the complicated and confusing streets of our nation's capital.

I was also starting to fall in love with my job and really getting to know the dealers in my territory, which specifically was all of Maryland, Washington, DC, Virginia, and part of North Carolina. The job mainly consisted of calling on my seventeen Harley-Davidson dealers and discussing with them the many different retail and wholesale programs that we were involved with at that particular time. The new Evolution engine was in five of our 1984 models, of which the most popular was the Softtail. It was called a Softtail because instead of having shock absorbers on the rear end, it had hidden shock absorbers underneath the transmission. This gave it the appearance of an old-style motorcycle on which bikers would eliminate the shock absorbers on the rear end and directly weld the frame together. That was called a hard tail. This motorcycle was very retro looking, and I think the company was banking on this particular model as well as the Evolution engine. Still, it was hard to sell dealers any new motorcycles, as they still had up to two years' worth of inventory on their showroom floor.

Most of the ones I worked with were stereotypical dealers who either inherited the business from their parents or worked in the dealership and somehow managed to scrape up enough money to buy it from the previous owner. They, as well as their staff, were usually uneducated but overachievers. These were the hard-working people who define America. And the business process by which Harley-Davidson operated was truly a free-enterprise system. The dealers bought the product from Harley at a price and turned around and sold it for whatever price they could possibly get. During these times, that wasn't much. Many of my dealers were poor as church mice. Most of them had tiny facilities that were no more than two to three thousand square feet. Their showrooms and storage areas were jam-packed with motorcycles, handlebar to handlebar. Most of these dealers were barely making ends meet, and in the 1980s, the interest rates for both retail and wholesale were nearly 20 percent. The typical margin, as suggested by Harley corporate, was only 25 percent. And so there was the struggle—trying to make a gross profit of five cents on every dollar. And then, of course, you had to pay the bills, which included monstrous interest payments. Even though I was happy to have this great job, I wondered why I hadn't studied the industry and the market more closely.

In January of 1985, I attended the annual Northeast Harley-Davidson Dealer Association winter meeting. This was a benign group of dealers who would have annual or semiannual meetings to discuss issues they were facing in the retail arena as well as their relationships with Harley-Davidson Motor Company. It was held somewhere near Philadelphia in some obscure little hotel that I barely remember. It was fun meeting—mainly drinking and camaraderie, with a few speakers and statistics thrown in for good measure. It was a typical group meeting including buffet dinners, and that is where I met a couple other dealers who were not in my territory—Bert from Philadelphia and Anthony from Long Island. I would later get to know these guys pretty well. The only other thing I remember from that get-together is meeting a group of girls, and one in particular who I ended up taking back to my hotel room. But before I took her to my room, Bert and Anthony made a bet with Hal that there was no way I could get her to do that. Hal won the bet, and as I walked past the entrance to the bar with this girl, I could see Bert and Anthony paying up.

Daytona Bike Week is the pride and joy of Harley-Davidson. It appears to just happen, but there is a lot of planning and coordination that goes into bringing 100,000 bikers into a sleepy little city and keeping them entertained for ten days. It took a few dozen employees from Harley corporate and a handful of the East Coast district managers to make Daytona Bike Week a success. The district managers were basically slaves under the direction of the corporate employees. It started with unloading the motorcycles and thousands of boxes and continued with creating an exciting event for our retail customers. We were at our stations at eight a.m.; worked until we were done, which could be as late as nine p.m.; hit the bars until closing; and then started all over again.

I was beginning to realize that I not only had the best job in the company, but I also had the worst job in the company! Aside from all the work, we had to talk to retail customers face-to-face during the entire day, including our time off at night in the bars. There was no escape. Some of that was fun, and I got to meet a lot of girls who wanted to hook up. But every once in a while, you would meet a retail customer who was a real pain in the ass. I remember one guy in particular who was half drunk and demanded an explanation for why the Motor Company had discontinued the kickstart feature on the motorcycles in favor of electric starters. I was having a little problem with this guy when Hal stepped in and said, "Hey, it's the same reason that cars don't have starter cranks anymore!" Then he told the guy to get the hell out of here.

As we were finishing up my first Daytona rally, all the district managers got a phone call asking us to report for an emergency meeting to discuss wholesale sales. Every district manager around the country flew to Milwaukee and met at a little town west of the city. I was on my way to attend what I would later find out was called a "boiler room." It was a meeting where all the sales force got together in one room for as long as it took to sell motorcycles at wholesale to our dealers. The retail pipeline was full, and I quickly learned why it was called a boiler room. We were not going to leave until we sold the number of wholesale motorcycles necessary to meet our financial projections to the banks. Remember, at this time, the dealer showrooms were still filled with motorcycles—some of them several years old, yet brand new. The dealers did not want more inventory. The first morning we all walked into the room and found conference tables set up in the U-shaped position. Every seat had a telephone, a district manager's name, a stack of cards with dealer information, and a thick blue binder with your dealers' history of retail wholesale and current inventory. Basically, our job was to jam more motorcycles down their throats. The meeting started with Vaughn Beals addressing the group and telling us that we would not leave this room until every motorcycle that had to be sold was sold. He had such a commanding presence, I immediately felt dedicated. I was about to learn a lot.

After a couple days of begging and using every selling skill that I had in my repertoire, I was at about the 50 percent mark, which also represented number fifteen out of thirty district managers. I was terribly disappointed and walked over to one of the veteran district managers, Ray, and asked him how he was doing so well. I'll never forget the way Ray looked at me and said, "I believe in God, and I never lie to my dealers!" I didn't think much of it at the time, but now I understand. Every time I see Ray, I tell him how much that moment changed my life. The only mental decision I made during that boiler room was that I needed some reason to actually love every dealer I had. I liked them, sure. But to translate what Ray had said into something that would work for me, I had to really find something that I loved about each and every dealer/ customer in my territory.

There were two dealers in my territory who were very active in the anti-Harley-Davidson Dealer Alliance Group, and as an employee, I really disliked them. One of them was a hillbilly who loved to hunt. The other was a good businessman who also had his pilot's license. They were both in Virginia, one in Elkhorn, the other in Dumfries. I loved to hunt, and I always had respect for anyone who could learn how to fly. With that small bit of information from Ray, a little bit of selling skill, and a lot of ambition, I ended up selling the third most motorcycles, at wholesale, to my dealers.

The whole theme of this boiler room was called the Hallelujah Package. It was so stupid, because it was based on selling radios and tour packs for the motorcycle in inventory that was selling at the slowest pace, the FXRT. As a dealer, if you bought enough motorcycles from us, especially the FXRT, you could win a trip for two to Hawaii. In addition to the success I had during my first boiler room, I was also very excited because the district managers would be flying to Hawaii to entertain the dealers who had won the Hallelujah Hawaii trip.

During the rest of that year, we had several boiler rooms trying to save the company by padding the financial statements and showing that the corporation had attained its wholesale shipment goals, all at the expense of the unsuspecting dealers who were ill-prepared to have more inventory shoved onto their showroom floors. In that year, there was even a district manager who, I think, almost had a nervous breakdown under the pressure of trying to convince his dealers to take more inventory. Obviously, during that time, there were many areas of the country that were experiencing a great economic downturn. The Northeast happened to be the area that I was in, and it was doing the best in the nation. That district manager ended up in another department. He later went on to be in charge of the Harley-Davidson demo fleet that took the current models all around the country by truck to let customers test-ride the motorcycles. Great for him!

I finally found a house in Virginia near Fredericksburg that was brand-new and affordable to me. It really was central in my territory, if you looked at the map. I think it was $54,200 for a three-bedroom one-bath two-story house butted up against a huge forest preserve. I asked a girl I had been dating in Milwaukee by the name of Anne to come out and move in with me. She was a dental assistant and found a job immediately in downtown Fredericksburg and became friends with one of the other assistants by the name of Lisa. Lisa was crazy! One night after a little bit of partying, she blurted out in a voice that sounded like Thurston Howell III from *Gilligan's Island*, "I want to suck your cock!" This was in front of her fiancé and in front of my girlfriend, and in the middle of a restaurant! In fact, her exact words were, "I want to suck your cock until my lips turn blue!" I was mortified. Her fiancé was mortified. But no one did anything about it. No one even brought it up again. We went to a party at their house celebrating one of the big three horseraces. They had purchased bushels and bushels of raw clams. During the middle of the party, she started running around the house screaming at her fiancé that she needed cocaine. Again, remember, this is in a female voice of Thurston Howell III screaming, "Sony, I need cocaine!"

During that year, things had started to pick up in the economy and in the motorcycle industry. Through the district managers' hard work and the dealers' sacrifice, the top hundred dealers and all the district managers had won an all-inclusive Caribbean cruise. The cruise was just what the doctor ordered, for me at least. It had been a tough year, with dealers struggling and upper management trying to get control of a company that was not modern, in a modern world. One of my dealers, Devin in Maryland, asked me if he could invite Eric Buell, who was trying to buy engines from Harley-Davidson with little success. One of the upper executives was absolutely opposed to selling parts and accessories to anyone except a Harley-Davidson dealer. I made the decision to let Devin invite Eric Buell on the trip in an effort to bring Eric and Jeff face to face so they could discuss some type of mutual relationship. Eventually, that did work out. And not long after that, Harley-Davidson and Buell went into partnership.

The cruise was a lot of fun and fairly uneventful. It was a rather short five days. It was in October, and we experienced storms that had waves crashing over the top of the ship. I have never seen so many sick people in my life. It's funny how odd a person looks when he or she is extremely ill. The most beautiful woman and the most handsome man can look like they have just walked out of a horror movie! The cruise-ship staff had lined the hand railings in the hallway with vomit bags about every ten feet. Nevertheless, the cruise was fun, and we even had entertainment from the *Saturday Night Live* guy who used to do the news on the show. Unfortunately, he only had one show to give and was going to give two performances. So, night number two was a big bomb for him.

After we docked in Miami, the dealers went home and the district managers boarded buses for an extended trip for several days in Key West, Florida. During that trip, close to the last day, I got up one morning to have breakfast and Hal and I decided we were going to go out for a day full of activities while our significant others went shopping, laid by the pool, or did whatever they wanted to do. So after breakfast, our morning started with MTV on, blaring these lyrics: "Money for nothing and chicks for free!" We were jumping up and down on the bed in his room and playing air guitar to this song when Hal's wife came in and screamed at us to get the hell out of the hotel room.

Hal and I decided to go and rent a catamaran and went out for about an hour. While we were sailing, Hal described to me his love for sailing but fear of sharks. As our time was nearly up and we are heading back toward shore and the place we had rented the catamaran, we caught a real gust of wind that pushed one of the pontoons into the water and flipped the catamaran. We went ass over tin cup! As I came out of the water, Hal was screaming, "Oh my God, sharks! Get me out of here!" Everything was A-OK, and we managed to clamber back on board and head back slowly to the vendor who had rented us the catamaran.

Then we decided to rent a couple of Jet Skis and take them out for a ride. We went to the office, checked in, showed them our identification, and paid for an hour of rental. The guy came out, gave us brief instructions, gave us our life-preserver jackets, and led us to the Jet Skis that were anchored about fifty yards out in shallow water. As we were wading out, I decided I should dive into the water to get wet, so that I wouldn't be cold once I got onto the splashing Jet Ski. So as everyone does when they jump in the ocean, I took a running start and with hands over my head took a dive—and hit a coral reef! The reef splayed my fingers as well as my arms, and I hit it with all of my body weight directly on the top of my head. It felt like I got hit on the head by a baseball bat swung by a Major League baseball player. As I was only in three feet of water, I staggered to my feet. You know how bad a head wound bleeds. You understand that water makes an easy conduit for it to flow. Within one second, my entire torso was covered in blood!

All that Hal heard was a noisy splash in the water. He turned around and to his surprise saw his buddy covered with blood and immediately assumed, fueled by his fear of sharks, that I had been attacked. As loud as he could scream, he was yelling, "Bob, Bob, Bob, shark, shark, shark!" At this point, I was as close to passing out as I have ever been. I managed to stay conscious, and Hal helped me to shore where there was a plethora of bystanders who had rushed to help the victim of the shark. I was indeed covered with blood from head to toe as I came from the water. It must have been a horrible sight.

As I was helped to shore by many people, someone came out to put a towel on my head to stop the bleeding. Thankful as I was, as they put pressure on my head, the pain in my neck was excruciating! It felt like someone had cut my back and placed a piece of burning charcoal in my neck. As the reality of the situation was starting to hit me, I also think the pain was starting to affect me physically. I started getting very faint. All of a sudden, and I'm not kidding, someone came out of the crowd and grabbed my hands. I couldn't see who it was because that towel was still draped over my head, but all I can tell you is she had those fluffy pants that many older women wear on the beach. She took my hands and with her thumbs started to gently rub the spot between my thumb and forefinger on both hands, and I immediately came to full consciousness. Instead of calling an ambulance, Hal and I opted for a cab. In the hospital for diagnosis and emergency repair, the final diagnosis was that I had broken my neck and was lucky to be alive and moving. Within an hour after coming out of observation and intensive care, Hal brought me a six-pack of beer and we celebrated life!

CHAPTER 4

THE LIBERTY RIDE

EVERY DISTRICT MANAGER is responsible for his territory and everything that goes on within it. If there is an event that has anything to do with Harley-Davidson, the district manager has a responsibility to, at a minimum, attend the event and most likely be in complete charge of everything that happens. In 1986, Lee Iacocca was heading up the national and international campaign for the rejuvenation of the Statue of Liberty. Harley-Davidson jumped on the bandwagon and initiated motorcycle rides all around the country to gather donations from the riders. Vaughn Beals was leading a ride from Milwaukee that was stopping in Washington, DC, prior to the final trip to Ellis Island, where he would present the check of the donations gathered from the ride to Lee Iacocca. For this special event, Harley-Davidson had produced a limited number of motorcycles bearing a Statue of Liberty emblem. All of the executives had full dressers that were silver and gray. As the district manager for the Washington, DC, area, I was responsible for leading the ride from the northwest corner of Virginia into Washington, DC, and then through Maryland and into Pennsylvania.

I didn't have much money at the time, and I didn't have a lightweight leather jacket for the ride. I couldn't even afford a Harley-Davidson leather jacket, so I went to the local mall and went to Wilsons Leathers. There I found a lightweight leather sport coat. It was a little bit fancy, but I really couldn't find anything else that I could afford. The first time Vaughn Beals saw me, he said I was the most dapper motorcyclist he had ever seen! I really felt like an idiot.

We got to Washington, DC, and I was informed by Buck in our public relations department that he had promised my motorcycle to someone from the press. I asked him what he expected me to do, and he just looked at me as if I was an idiot. In the middle of the hotel lobby, I read him the riot act. I hadn't been that pissed off in a long time! I wanted to beat this skinny little piece of crap into the ground. I had to find a motorcycle somewhere in my territory within twelve hours if I was going to continue to lead the ride. Miraculously, one of the dealers from North Carolina, Moe and his wife, were having some personal issues and needed to fly back to their dealership immediately. We made arrangements for me to borrow their motorcycle for the rest of the trip and have it shipped back to them when the ride was done.

On the way up Interstate 95 in Pennsylvania very near the New Jersey, Delaware, New York border, the entire group stopped at a wayside for a gas and bathroom break. Unfortunately, I was one of the last ones to leave the rest station, and in an attempt to catch up to the front of the group, I rode as fast as I could in the emergency lane on the right-hand side of the highway. I ended up taking a nail in the rear tire and had to pull over, park the bike on the side of one of the busiest highways in the United States, and leave it there. Everything I had for that trip was packed away in the motorcycle, so all I could do was lock it and leave it. Now what to do? I stuck my thumb out and started hitchhiking.

Almost immediately, I was picked up by a woman riding a BMW. She graciously gave me a ride to the next rest stop. At that rest stop, I was explaining my circumstances to a group of bikers and one tough-looking biker offered me a ride to Ellis Island on the back of his hard tail. About three miles after we left the rest stop, a skanky woman pulled up next to us on her hard-tail Harley and this guy yelled to her, "Hey, Alice, look what I got for you!" Within two seconds, she lifted up her shirt, showing me her tits, and gave her friend and me the thumbs-up. I was thinking that I was to be kidnapped and never seen or heard from again. As soon as we got to the Ellis Island parking lot, I bolted as fast as I could. I never saw them again.

After the presentation of the check from Vaughn Beals to the Statue of Liberty Foundation, Hal and I took a quick ride back to get my motorcycle. It was gone. So the district managers, Hal, George, and I headed over to a local hotel to coordinate the retrieval and return of the executives' motorcycles back to Milwaukee. We shuttled a few motorcycles over to the local dealership and by nighttime realized that the public-relations department, which hadn't communicated with us, had journalists on these bikes all over town. So we went to the bar to drink. And drink we did! I remember specifically drinking these tall boots of beer. Really, the glass was one foot tall and shaped like a boot. That and a couple of shots of Jack Daniels, and it was off to bed and then to track these motorcycles down early in the morning.

The next morning was a cluster fuck! These liberal journalists had left the bikes unattended all over the parking lot without any direction on where to leave the keys, and some of them actually left the keys in the ignition of the motorcycle. Our public-relations guys, Buck, was an idiot. We finally found all the keys and delivered all the motorcycles to the local dealership, and after George left, Al and I decided to go into Manhattan. I had Vaughn Beals's motorcycle, and during the late afternoon rush hour as we were heading into Manhattan, the beer and the Jack Daniels hit my bladder and lower bowels. We were stuck in rush-hour traffic and I had to piss, right now! I signaled to Hal and we pulled off to the side of the freeway. I unzipped my pants and bent down, pretending to check something on the motorcycle. As I was taking a leak, as most men do, I gave it one last squeeze to finish off my piss and shit in my pants! Oh boy, here I was with crap in my pants on the side of New York City's busiest freeway with no idea what I was going to do. Remember, the motorcycle with all my clothes had been left on the side of the highway. I start yelling to Hal to help me out and that I had crapped in my pants, and all he did was start to laugh and get the camera out of his tour pack. He came over and started taking pictures as I was screaming obscenities. He ended up finding a discarded Wendy's restaurant bag, and that's what I used to clean myself. Very embarrassing. I wonder if anyone reading this was on that freeway at that time and saw us.

Before we got back on the bikes, I told Hal that we needed to find the first McDonald's restaurant that we could so I could do a proper job of cleaning myself. He informed me there were no bathrooms in the restaurants in New York City. I didn't believe him. He was right. So we headed over to the Twin Towers. It was just starting to rain, and we decided that it would be a great place to have a couple of drinks, relax, and figure out what we were going to do the next day to get back my motorcycle. When we got to the parking structure, I tried to argue with the attendant, who wanted to charge fifteen dollars per motorcycle for us to park, even as I was emphatic that we would park both motorcycles in one space. I had no luck, so we paid thirty dollars to park and headed up to the bar on the top floor. It was raining and overcast, so we had absolutely no view and decided to have a couple quick drinks and head over to Long Island, stay with our friend and dealer Anthony for the night, and try to get my motorcycle in the morning. As we left the parking lot, I hit the median just right, and it happened to be the exact length of the width between my front and rear wheel. I slid sideways on Vaughn Beals's motorcycle, hopping and skipping until I nearly dislocated my shoulder. But the bike never went down.

We took the ferryboat over to Long Island and went to Anthony's house, which was an apartment above a dealership. We got a couple of bottles of booze and drank and talked all night long. One of our conversations was about the fact that I would never get my motorcycle from the New Jersey Turnpike Authority without the proper paperwork. In my naïveté, I told them I would simply show them my driver's license and my business card and I was sure I would be successful in retrieving the motorcycle. We got up the next morning and, after calling and finding out where my motorcycle was, got into Anthony's Porsche 911. Being the youngest, although the biggest, I had to crawl into the back window space. It had rained all night and the roads were wet—and the roads on Long Island, with all the parked cars, are basically one-way streets. Anthony drove that Porsche like he was in the Indy 500! I was scared to death.

We got to the New Jersey Turnpike Authority station where my motorcycle was impounded, and it was just like they had explained to me. We walked in and sitting behind a one-inch plate-glass window was a big fat patrolman with a cigar in his mouth and his feet up on the counter. I showed him my ID and my business card and explained that he had my motorcycle and I was there to retrieve it. He asked me if I had any paperwork, and I tried to explain that it was a company-owned vehicle and we didn't have any paperwork. Through that thick glass window and with the cigar in the corner of his mouth, he said, "If you ain't got no paperwork, then you ain't gettin' no motorcycle!" In the meantime, Hal and Anthony had gone to the restroom, and I had a feeling they were snorting something. Also laughing their asses off! I was successful in begging the trooper to allow me to get a change of clothes and fresh underwear out of the motorcycle. I figured that Harley-Davidson Motor Company, in its infinite wisdom, could figure out how to get the motorcycle back from the New Jersey Turnpike Authority. I got on the next plane back to Washington, DC.

CHAPTER 5

MY FIRST HARLEY-DAVIDSON TRIP THROUGH EUROPE

At a district-manager conference, one of our speakers was a man from our international department located in Connecticut. His name was Len, and he was the vice president of international sales for Harley-Davidson Motor Company. At dinner that evening, after Len had talked about the problems with black-market sales of used motorcycles in Europe, we ended up sitting at the same dinner table. Len was quite a drinker, and after several hours of conversation he invited me to go to Europe and use a motorcycle from Harley-Davidson GmbH in Frankfurt. GmbH is a German term meaning corporation or the corporation.

I was a little bit nervous even applying for my passport. But I really thought that a trip through Europe on a Harley would be the cat's ass and fulfill a dream of a lifetime. I bought maps of Europe and took out my German book from high school and started studying every night. I studied for forty-five days while I was waiting for my passport to arrive from Washington, DC. I used my Frequent Flyer points to get the airline ticket and set aside about a thousand dollars for a one-week trip. The day before I was to leave, I still hadn't received my passport! I called the Washington, DC, passport agency and, believe it or not, got a wonderful government agent on the phone who assured me that my passport had been mailed the day before and I should receive it in the morning. My flight was set to leave late in the afternoon from Washington, DC, to John F. Kennedy Airport in New York and subsequently to Frankfurt. I received the passport at eleven a.m., which was only four hours before my flight was to depart.

The flight from Washington, DC, was delayed and arrived at JFK airport late, and the flight to Frankfurt had already departed. The airline made arrangements for me to stay in a local hotel, but there was another issue. I was supposed to leave on a Thursday but was now scheduled to depart on Friday, which meant I would arrive on Saturday morning, and GmbH is closed on Saturdays. That meant I couldn't pick up my motorcycle until Monday. With the six-hour time difference, I had to try to contact Klaus, who was the managing director of GmbH for all of Europe. He also happened to know my brother Eddie, thank goodness, and had been contacted by Len who informed him to extend me all the courtesies of any executive from Harley-Davidson. When I was finally able to reach Klaus, all that he said over the phone was a phrase I was to learn was common from the Europeans and especially the Germans: "No problem!"

After an uneventful night in a hotel in the middle of

nowhere (even though it was near downtown New York), I successfully departed on my five p.m. flight and arrived in Frankfurt at seven in the morning. Klaus had given me his home address and told me to come to his house. The taxi ride was $115! And that was back in the mid-1980s. I arrived at his home exhausted, and he and his wife treated me with the utmost European hospitality. He immediately explained to me that he had his son take the motorcycle from GmbH on Friday and ride it to his home so that I could pick it up and begin my vacation—or holiday, as the Europeans call it.

Even though it was ten o'clock in the morning, Klaus brought me a good German beer and offered me some snacks as we sat on his backyard patio overlooking what appeared to be a nature sanctuary. There were birds of every type flying in to feast on the bird feeders that he and his wife had erected. She talked about how proud she was that she could attract so many different types of birds to her bird feeders. Klaus asked me where I wanted to go, and I showed him my pre-marked map. All he could say, in his deep German-sounding English voice, was, "No, no, no!" He added, "I will show you the best trip that you can take on a motorcycle through Europe in seven days!" He took my well-thought-out and marked-up map and, with an indelible marker, rewrote my entire trip. He started out by saying that he would take me to a small town celebrating its 950th anniversary, and where he had some friends who had a boat, and I could stay with them on the first night.

Klaus and I rode our motorcycles on a beautiful countryside road all the way to this little town near Frankfurt, and he introduced me to the owners of the boat who were also his friends. There were two guys and a girl named Hannah. I felt a little uncomfortable, because it was a very small boat and I had already agreed to spend the night with all of them. It was only five o'clock in the afternoon, and I immediately started to wonder what the sleeping arrangements would be. The name of the boat was the Sherry Express. I quickly found out that it was called that because the owner loved to drink sherry, and plenty of it. We had a few drinks on the boat and then Klaus left on his motorcycle for home. My three new stranger/friends took me to the local monastery, where the monks had brewed a special beer just for the town's anniversary. It was some of the best and freshest dark beer I have ever had in my life! We all drank quite a bit. I can't imagine how they felt after mixing Sherry and beer, but in the morning after sleeping outside, on the boat, on the foldout seats, I certainly wasn't feeling very good.

After we exchanged addresses and I said my good-byes in my best German, I got on my motorcycle and headed over to Heidelberg. Once again, the ride was very beautiful, and I was amazed by how many of the farmers were still cultivating their land by hand and not by tractor. I passed many a farm where the workers, including women in babushkas and long dresses, were working the fields with pitchforks the size of snow shovels. There wasn't a little town that I rode through or stopped in that the inhabitants didn't come to the curb, if there was a curb, and stare at me as I rode by. It's kind of amazing when you go to areas where people have not seen a Harley-Davidson motorcycle very often, what an impact this truly magnificent machine can make on someone. It never ceases to amaze me. In Heidelberg, I found a small hotel called Hotel am Schloss, which was at the bottom of the ruins of one of the biggest castles in Germany. In English, the hotel name was "hotel by the castle." I toured that castle the next morning through the afternoon, and little did I know that this would be the first time of five times I would visit.

I wandered my way over to France, but because of the times, I needed a visa to visit or enter France. Screw the French! When I tried to enter through the customs checkpoint, they stopped me and tore apart every square inch of my luggage and my motorcycle. And naturally, they would not let me into their country. Once again, screw the French!

Again I took a beautiful ride through the Black Forest south toward Munich heading into Switzerland, with a final destination of Zurich. I had not made any reservations and looked for a hotel room in the center of town. I found one that was a perfect location for me to spend the next day walking around this beautiful city on the river sightseeing and window-shopping. I met a girl in a coffee shop by the name of Sofia. She was a very pretty Swiss girl. We spent the night having dinner, drinking, dancing, and making love, right up until I had to check out of the hotel. Naturally, and as usual, we exchanged phone numbers and addresses, both well knowing that we would never see each other again.

The route to Innsbruck, Austria, is by far my favorite motorcycle trip on earth. You ride through mountain foothills, gullies, and grasslands. Some of the hairpin turns had my floorboards shooting sparks three feet long.

When you enter Innsbruck, the mountains abruptly stop in the middle of this beautiful little village that is probably the storybook version of what Europe is like. I found a hotel on the outskirts of town, spent the night, toured the city, and left the next morning on my way to Germany.

On my way back to Frankfurt, winding through the beautiful German countryside, I stopped in a little village called Michelstadt, which means "the city of Michel." Even though I knew it was foolish, I felt, very deep inside, like this was where I came from. In the town center, I had a sandwich for lunch and wrote every one of my family members a postcard expressing my feelings about finding the roots of what possibly could have been our familial origins.

One of the people who worked for Klaus was a guy by the name of Hans. He was the public-relations manager for GmbH. He took me to his home when I arrived back in Frankfurt, after I had dropped the motorcycle off the night before I was to depart for America. He and his wife had a newborn baby, and when I arrived at the door of their house, Hans and his wife came down to greet me with the baby in her arms. The baby farted as we were exchanging introductions, and in German, she said to the baby, "Oh, Sie sprechen Französisch?" This means, "Oh, are you speaking French?" Very fitting and appropriate!

It was such a wonderful adventure, and I can't thank my friend Klaus enough for his redirection of my adventure as well as going the extra mile to bring my motorcycle to his home, entertain me, and take me to the first stop of what was not my first destination but the beginning of my journey. That's where that phrase comes from—"It's not the destination, it's the journey!" As many motorcycle trips as I have taken in my life, that first one through Europe by myself will always be the single most memorable experience that I will keep deep in my heart and soul.

CHAPTER 6

THE GLORY DAYS

THE DISTRICT MANAGERS, DURING the tough times, worked every event that was anywhere near our territory. Being on the East Coast, I was responsible for and required to work Daytona Bike Week every year. Daytona was a special event—in fact, it was very special. I remember one of the secretaries to Vaughn Beals, a woman by the name of Brenda, introducing me to—with the intention of hooking me up with— this young, beautiful British woman working at the Muscular Dystrophy Association donation table. She was extremely beautiful, with long blonde hair and bright blue eyes. I ended up walking over, and her handshake had me convinced to ask her out for the evening. This was tricky, as my fellow district managers, most of them married, expected us all to go out as a group and get our buzz on.

When I opened the door, this beautiful woman walked in … along with her ass that was the size of Cleveland! I had only seen her sitting down behind a table. When we were through, after an excruciating evening out, we went back to my hotel room and I couldn't even think about asking her into the room. She forced her way in, and the best I could do was to let her go down on me for a blow job, because there was no way, physically, in my mind, that we could fuck! The sheer mechanics of trying to make love to her were impossible.

Over the next two years, I had plenty of opportunities for sexual exploits. Like the time I was rooming with Howard and one of his employees came to our room, and I ended up screwing her in the bathroom while her boss was sleeping (or maybe listening from his bed). I actually think her hair ended up getting wet in the toilet as I was doing her from behind. My dealer from Washington, DC, had a fifty-four-foot scarab racing boat. He took me out on the boat a few times all around Chesapeake Bay. He invited me to meet a girl who apparently had met me at one of his dealership events and wanted to have sex with me. We took the boat all around the Chesapeake and I ended up fucking her on the back seat of cushions on the race boat. There was another girl who I met at a gas station near my house, and after finding out that I worked for Harley, she came right out and said that she wanted to go to my house and screw. There were so many others, and I remember one in particular, just because I met her at McDonald's and had to talk to her because her keychain had a large tag on it that said, "Wine Me, Dine Me, 69 Me!" I think she fucked me harder than any woman had ever fucked me before.

And then there was the time in Atlanta when all the district managers had been called together for a boiler room to sell, or jam, motorcycles down our dealers' throats. A lot of the guys were into hiring hookers. I wasn't, relying instead on my good looks and charm. Ha-ha! This one hooker was very beautiful, and a few of the district managers hired her to come to their individual rooms. In the meantime, my friend Bart left early after negotiating a deal with another hooker. As I got back to the room and opened the door, an ugly black woman came to the door to greet me. Thank goodness I got there when I did, because Bart was passed out with his pants around his ankles, and this black hooker was rummaging through his belongings. This consummate saleswoman actually asked me if I wanted any action. All I could say was "No … But, thank you! Please leave the room."

During that period of the early and mid-'80s, being the district manager was simply a matter of trying to sell the dealers every motorcycle that was coming off the end of the production line. The dealer showrooms were still full of prior model year motorcycles, and our job as district sales managers was to keep the pipeline of wholesale motorcycles clean.

It was the middle of June 1987, and my brother Tommy really wanted to buy a new Harley-Davidson. During that period of time, the FXRT, although it was Vaughn Beals's favorite motorcycle, was the worst-selling motorcycle in our inventory. The Motor Company had dramatically discounted that motorcycle to the dealers just to get rid of the inventory they had produced. I convinced one of my dealers in Washington, DC, to buy an extra one, strip it down, and turn it into a simple low-rider. He did that and I got my brother a rape of a deal—actually, he only paid about four thousand dollars for it after all the discounts.

He and his wife drove out in their little pickup truck and stayed with me for a couple of days, drinking ourselves blind; we loaded the motorcycle up in the back of the pickup truck and they headed home. He still has that motorcycle to this day, and it is in perfect condition!

Shortly after that, I was already packed and prepared to visit my stepsister, Mary, in Boston for the weekend. I got a phone call from one of my dealers in Virginia, and the phone call actually was from Pinky the office manager. She informed me that there was a problem and that Dan, the owner, had checked himself into a hospital. I asked her what the problem was, and all she said was there was a problem with the inventory. I asked her if that was the same inventory I had just checked the week before, and she said yes. And I asked her if all the bikes were there, and she answered no. So I said, "So the inventory I took was not accurate, is that correct?"

And she said, "Yes, Bob! There is a problem!"

My heart sank. In those days, the district managers were responsible for the entire inventory in their territory and for confirming every motorcycle that the dealers had floor-planned with ITT Financial. That was the credit division that provided motorcycles for the dealers when Harley-Davidson would not send the motorcycles to the dealers on a thirty-day open invoice. I called my stepsister, canceled our plans, and immediately drove to Virginia to intervene in this dealer problem, which is called "sold out of trust." That is when a dealer sells motorcycles and does not pay the creditor—either Harley-Davidson or in most cases during those years ITT—on a timely basis (usually five to seven days).

I spent the next thirty days trying to sort things out. The dealer had checked himself into a mental institution, and his schoolteacher wife took time off work trying to help sort things out. It was to no avail, because the dealership owed hundreds of thousands of dollars not only to the Motor Company and ITT Financial but also in back taxes and many other bills. At one point, when I could finally explain all the details, his wife passed out and fell on the floor. Thank God for her parents, who were there in support and could take care of her. I also had a guy, a big black guy, come in and say that he owned ten Sportsters. At that time, we didn't have the Harley-Davidson lawyers involved, so I asked him to show me proof. He produced ten Manufacturer's Certificates of Origin, or as we call them, MCOs. I told him that was not proof of ownership because H-D prints those, and they'll just print ten more. I suggested that he contact his attorney immediately.

I ended up selling the dealership for the debt that was owed to ITT. So for $110,000, a guy by the name of Jim, who also owned a couple of car dealerships, bought the dealership for a song. I also saved my job by the grace of John Finstad. As my asshole boss was on an extended vacation, John stepped in and convinced ITT, which would always wield unlimited power over the district managers and almost all of the dealers, that I had done my due diligence to correct my wrongdoing. After the closing of the sale of the dealership, which only took thirty days, Wendel, the president of the ITT branch of Harley-Davidson Financial, called me and told me that my stock in his eyes had risen to an incredible high.

Almost immediately after that, I was informed that I had a new boss. Wayne had been a district manager in the Florida area. Prior to that, he was a mechanic at his father's dealership, and he was also best friends with the director of sales, David. I thought that Wayne was a nerd, and everyone in our district had a nickname for him: Pencil Neck. My stepmother would sarcastically refer to him as Eberhard (Eberhard is the name of a pencil). That always made me chuckle. Wayne and I went on to become good friends. During the mid-1980s, Harley had a great human resources ideology of hiring into the company based on employee referrals. H-R personnel changed and so did logical hiring and promoting practices. It was a little annoying to see that you didn't need to be good at your job to get promoted as long as you were friends with the boss. This became a more common theme the longer I stayed and worked at Harley-Davidson. If you kissed the boss's ass, you would get promoted. Harley-Davidson had transformed from the nepotism of the Davidsons to the political arena of ass-kissing.

I had gone fishing with David and some of our friends from Harley-Davidson on Lake Erie. More specifically, we fished from our base camp on Put-in-Bay. I never considered this as ass-kissing because it was just a bunch of guys who loved to fish. The last time I went, I met a girl by the name of Bernice. Herman was a district manager from Iowa, and he was one of our fishing buddies. I borrowed his minivan so that I could have sex with Bernice in the back of the van. She was a very pretty girl, and all the guys were jealous. When Herman found out that I had sex in his van, he was furious and refused to talk to me for several months.

During my last year as a district manager, the dealer show for the 1989 model year motorcycles was held in Baltimore, which was part of my territory. I didn't have much responsibility except to make sure that my district manager brethren were shown the best spots to eat, drink, and enjoy strip clubs. One night, I took the guys out to a strip club in the middle of Baltimore and everyone who wanted to get laid could get laid. I ended up with a stripper who walked all the way to my hotel in her stage outfit, which consisted of a white wedding dress and white lace gloves that went up to her elbows. I was very embarrassed when she walked into the lobby and I escorted her to the elevator and into my room. We had sex for several hours, and I was completely ready for her to ask me for a couple hundred dollars. She didn't.

The times were changing, and the politics and the paperwork for the district managers was becoming ridiculous. As the company started doing better, there were more demands for the district managers to put less emphasis on sales and more emphasis on paperwork. Trust me; it still wasn't easy getting the dealers to accept motorcycles as the corporation produced more. The corporation was making a lot of profit, and you could see the greed in the eyes of the lower-level people in the organization just praying that they would be promoted if they could kiss the correct asshole. I really couldn't take it. I actually talked to my brother David, who owned multiple chiropractic practices, about coming to work for him as a consultant. But all of a sudden, a job opening became available for manager of store design. This person would be in charge of helping the dealers remodel their dealerships and upgrade their archaic showrooms to a modern retail environment. During one of our many district manager meetings throughout the year, we had a guest speaker by the name of Clark. He was a retail environment designer and specialist in the general area of retail sales. I really paid attention to what he was talking about and spent some time after his presentation discussing the job opening and how, in his opinion, I could get that job. I thought that he was an odd fellow, but he had a fantastic personality and a wealth of information that I really needed to help me get this job and get back to Milwaukee where my family was. I also thought that it would get me out from under the bullshit that was going on in the sales department.

The entire sales division was starting to get the idea that they were the greatest thing on earth. The fact is that in 1984, 1985, and 1986, that was true. But by now the country was coming out of a recession, with Ronald Reagan as president, and things were going along quite strongly. There is a great myth that when Ronald Reagan visited the York, Pennsylvania, Harley-Davidson plant and announced that because of the embargoes placed on the Asians, Harley-Davidson had attained success, Harley-Davidson announced that it no longer needed the embargoes, one year earlier than had been mandated by the government. The truth is that the "Buy American" philosophy/movement had already started to sweep the country. The gap between the Japanese yen and the American dollar had started to equalize. Japanese motorcycles were no longer cheap. All of the Japanese motorcycle dealerships in the United States had several years' worth of inventory, and they were in serious trouble. Harley corporate simply took advantage of a market situation and made it seem like it was their idea and that they had succeeded in their grand business scheme. On the contrary, it was pure luck and timing, like the market always is.

The person who was in charge of the new job opening reported directly to one of the VPs. That vice president was one of the upper executives, and I always thought that he was a mama's boy. No offense meant. I didn't like him, and I think that he never liked me. He said to me that if I could prove to him that I could change a penny into a nickel, he would buy my idea! The negotiation for my new position, including my salary and a motorcycle, took several days because I think the VP held him like a puppet on a string. We finally agreed on a salary that was approximately 25 percent less than what I was earning at the time. I accepted the job from a phone booth after making a dealer call somewhere out of Washington, DC. I was elated because I could go back to Milwaukee and be closer to my family.

I was informed the next day that my replacement would be a young man by the name of Joe. He had worked in the lower levels at Harley-Davidson, but his father had been a pillar in the organization for many years. My last assignment, before turning my territory over, was to help sell the dealership in Washington, DC. Jim and the manager of dealer development, Bob, came to Washington, DC, and we set up approximately twenty interviews for new dealers who wanted to purchase my good friend Howard's dealership, which was actually located near Washington,

DC, just southeast of the Beltway. We had two days of interviews and after they departed, I ended up in the bar and picked up a hooker. She came and sat next to me, as I was one of only three people in the bar. I asked her if she was working. She said yes. I asked how much? She said a buck. I said okay and gave her my room number. She arrived about five hours later, and I was too tired to do anything except asked her to give me a hand job. I wish I had those hundred dollars today.

I picked up Joe at the DC airport, and in the confusion I picked up luggage that I thought belonged to him. When we arrived at our hotel, I handed him his bag and he exclaimed that it wasn't his. We took the bag to my room and opened it up and found that it belonged to a woman, and there was enough information, along with panties and a dildo, to find out where she was staying in Washington, DC. I contacted her and by the end of the night had some of the greatest sex I'd had in a long time.

I took Joe to every one of my dealers and introduced him and tried to make my dealers comfortable with the new guy. That wasn't really easy, because the dealers were feeling and smelling the change that was in the air. Joe, or as I began to call him, Joe Joe, had a Porsche. So I figured he wouldn't mind if I drove very fast. I mean, after all, I had a Chrysler LeBaron GTS turbo. Well, a woman with a little road rage got me mad and so I decided, at about seventy-five miles an hour, to tap her bumper. I guess Joe Joe wasn't prepared for that, and he was screaming and yelling at me to slow down and stop what I was doing. I had a new job, I was going home, and that's life in the fast lane!

CHAPTER 7

BACK TO BEER TOWN

I spent about a month or two flying back and forth to Milwaukee, house hunting. I knew that I would be traveling a lot, and I decided upon a very large side-by-side duplex in Shorewood, which is a quaint suburb of Milwaukee approximately fifteen minutes from Harley corporate headquarters on Juneau Avenue. It was a beautiful Georgian colonial with two-story pillars. It had a three-car garage and was constructed in a brick that is called the Milwaukee brick. It is recycled brick that is a medium tan and black. Each side had three bedrooms and a bathroom upstairs, a large living room with fireplace, a dining room, a kitchen, and a full basement. I thought it was perfect, and it was located directly across the street from my childhood high school. I also felt comfortable knowing that someone would be around, at least living on the other side of the duplex, because I would be traveling extensively. I moved in June of 1988.

I jumped right in with both feet under the direction of my new boss. During this period of time, the vice president of sales, Jim Patterson, who was a great guy, was promoted to president of Harley-Davidson Motor Company. David was promoted to vice president of sales. Not necessarily a good thing, I thought, especially for the district managers, because David demanded ridiculously insignificant paperwork from the very people the corporation relied on to do nothing but produce sales and more specifically results. Moving into my office in the parts and accessories warehouse building was very strange after having an office in my home. I was now surrounded by 99 percent of coworkers who had never worked outside of the company. At least I had an office by myself, with a door. My main tutoring came from the consultant on design for Harley-Davidson, Clark. I give him all the credit for his teachings about store design and modern retail environment of the Harley dealerships today. Not only was he a mentor, but he turned out to be a great friend.

One of my new bosses had been a district manager, and so he understood the philosophy with which I was going to approach this position. It was going to take a lot of camaraderie with the district managers and a tremendous rapport with the dealers to convince them to spend hundreds of thousands of dollars to remodel their showrooms. At the time I was hired, only three dealers had been convinced to go through the remodeling process. The financial results, statistically, were outstanding. The average increase in parts and accessories sales (including general merchandise, which Harley-Davidson referred to as their clothing, trinkets, and trash), was over 300 percent. I realized that my greatest assets were my ability to sell, my rapport with the district managers, and the fact that I had an uncanny ability to remember almost every dealer's name in the United States. That was only about six hundred dealers. The ones I didn't know well, I got enough information from the district manager prior to meeting them and pretended that I had met them and knew all about them.

My closing ratio turned out to be 99 percent. Every dealer who I talked to about remodeling a store and the potential increase in sales signed up for the program. There were a couple who had weak district managers, and they were the few who didn't sign up for the program, with much regret. It was actually a simple sell. Spend $200,000 and increase your sales by $1 million. At a 25 percent margin, you would have paid for the remodeling in one year, plus any interest if you had to borrow the money from your bank. I don't want to brag, but I was good! The district managers loved me because I helped increase their parts and accessories and general merchandise numbers. The corporation loved me because I was helping the dealers increase their ancillary sales of our products times ten. The dealers loved me, after they hated me, for the increased profits they were making after remodeling. If you've ever gone through a remodel in your home, you can understand why they hated me for a while. That hatred passed very quickly when the cash registers were singing.

I was traveling six days a week, visiting every district manager who wanted me to visit any dealer who was interested in remodeling. I would leave the office late on Friday night, after returning from the Milwaukee airport. I would take care of my laundry, pay bills, mow the lawn, and depart Sunday for another ten domestic destinations that next week. I was signing up dealers faster than my single-man department could keep up with. I couldn't even return all my phone messages. That was in the days before the corporation allowed us to have cell phones. Small reminder to me about the small size of the world Harley lived in. And it reminded me of the fact that, pardon the expression, the corporation always wanted to reinvent the wheel. A case in point is the fact that the automobile industry had an outstanding computer system for dealer networks, but one of the upper executives at Harley decided to buy this tiny little company in Cleveland by the name of Cycom. It was the worst computer system for our dealer network that you could possibly imagine. He refused to acknowledge that he'd made a mistake, and to this day the system is riddled with problems.

Anyway, I was in Hawaii for a dealer-incentive award trip and was allowed to do a presentation to the top one hundred dealers about remodeling their dealerships. All dealers were required to attend, and Clark and I put on an outstanding presentation, with the normal dog-and-pony show of slides and statistics. After the presentation, we were overwhelmed with questions and requests for personal visits to their dealerships. A dealer from Milwaukee went up to one of the upper executives and told him, very matter-of-factly, "If you want this program to succeed, you better get Bob Michel more employees. Because if you don't, this program is never going to fly, and the dealers will get disappointed, and you know the dealers talk among themselves."

There was a girl from the computer company who was

also at the Hawaiian dealer presentation. Her name was Caroline, and she was a beautiful tall and thin woman with a wonderful personality. My boss made a special and specific request that I not go anywhere near her because he felt for her like he did his own daughter. I knew that he was an odd guy, but this one kind of took me by surprise. I ended up spending a very romantic evening with her, late at night, walking through the lava deserts of Hawaii under a full moon. Such a very special memory. By the time I got back to Milwaukee, I had the approval to hire two employees into my department. I went to work on that with reckless abandon. I had been working with a temp by the name of Jenny who was a little bit crazy. She had been recommended by a coworker who later became a district manager. She was an expert at merchandising, and that is what I needed to help the dealers with after they had remodeled their stores, to teach them how to properly display their merchandise in their newly remodeled and beautiful stores. She was very good, but she had a personality that, in her few visits to dealerships, had already brought a couple of complaints. When I had the opportunity to hire full-time people, with college degrees and vast experience, I wanted something better. I hired a woman by the name of Pam and another woman by the name of Shelley. They turned out to be my greatest assets and lifelong friends.

Shelley and I went to work at a store in Philadelphia. The owner, Brian, was a dealer I had met when I first became a district manager. We were accompanied by Clark, and Brian had done a perfect job of remodeling the store according to the specifications and blueprints. The evening after we had spent two days merchandising his store, he hired a limousine and took us all to downtown Philly to a very expensive Italian restaurant. It was a large group of people including his managers, Clark, Shelley, and myself. We were seated in an elevated area and were having one hell of a time drinking, laughing, and joking. We started to talk about the odd last names of people we know. I mentioned that I knew a guy by the name of Whip Koch. His father's name was Harry. We all laughed. I also knew a girl in high school by the name of Sandy Weiner. We all laughed again. And then Brian told us that his HOG chapter director was named Harry Ball. Without hesitation, my friend Clark raised his hand and at the same time as the restaurant grew quiet, he screamed out that he knew two Harry Balls! The entire restaurant, as well as the table, was silent for a moment. And then the entire establishment and all the patrons burst into laughter that was uncontrollable for several minutes. The fact is, he actually did know two men by that name.

The first year that I was in this position, the new model announcement show for the dealers was in San Francisco. It also happened to coincide with the same hotel as the National Gay Convention. Not that there's anything wrong with that. Jay Leno was going to be our main entertainment at the president's dinner, which was held on the last night of the dealer convention. I was very focused, because it was my first major presentation to a group of approximately five hundred people. As it turned out, all of the dealers brought their parts and accessories managers to the show, and it ended up being standing room only. Thank goodness Clark was there with me, and he actually led the presentation with my salesmanship as a sidekick. The dealers were lining up like sheep wanting to be the next in line to have their stores remodeled. I needed more employees. Jay Leno was fantastic. And I actually got to shake his hand. For an hour he joked about motorcycling and the addiction to being on the open road. That night I paid for a massage with a happy ending. I had been so focused on being a good corporate boy, and it turned out perfectly.

Another year went by traveling from state to state Sunday through Friday with little time for me to even mow the lawn or pay my bills. At that time, I was also taking care of my mom's house. I was living in the fast lane without the money. Fortunately my boss, Chuck, had arranged for me to receive stock options from my position. At that point, he was my greatest advocate in the company. However, Jim Patterson was leaving because of health problems. The board of directors elected Rich Teerlink as president. That was the single most important action that Harley-Davidson corporate had ever done in its history. Please read that again. Rich Teerlink turned out to be the greatest president that Harley-Davidson ever had.

I traveled and I traveled and I went from dealership to dealership selling the concept that if a dealer would remodel and spend the money, that dealer would reap financial rewards beyond all expectations. Motorcycle sales were going very well, and in fact, motorcycles were in demand. Harley was trying to ramp up production to meet the demand because dealers were starting to charge over manufacturer's suggested retail price. That is the free enterprise system. I didn't have a problem with that.

A lot of our customers did—but they sure didn't have a problem when we couldn't sell a motorcycle and they wanted it at rock-bottom price. It is called the law of supply and demand. Nothing on earth or in heaven above can change that basic economic principle. After Rich left the company, the new Harley-Davidson management started on a path thinking that it could do just that.

CHAPTER 8

TO RUSSIA (AND BACK) WITH LOVE

DURING THE SUMMER OF 1989, things at Harley-Davidson Motor Company were going extremely well. Sales were exceeding expectations, and everyone was busier than they ever expected to be. A few friends and I decided to take a motorcycle trip to Europe. We arranged to get some motorcycles from our European distributor in Frankfurt and take a trip from Germany to Holland, then to Denmark, up through Sweden, and over to Finland. Then we would go from Finland into Russia, specifically the city of Leningrad, which is now called St. Petersburg, back to Finland, then back to Sweden and down through Norway and back into Germany. The whole trip was to take us approximately two weeks.

The trip started in Frankfurt, early in the morning, and we headed off into Holland to meet with Josef, a friend of ours who had a dealership there. We had a very relaxed dinner and left the next morning for Copenhagen. The tulips in the dikes and the windmills in that area really were amazing to see. We loaded the motorcycles on a ferryboat and headed to southern Sweden. We made our way north to Oslo, spent the night with a local dealer, and boarded a ferryboat bound for Helsinki in the morning. It was approximately a twenty-four-hour trip, as I remember. The ferryboat was really like a floating casino. Or maybe even a cruise ship. It had all kinds of activities, including many bars and discotheques. A couple of us partied all night long. When we arrived in Helsinki in the morning, I was the last one off the boat. I was so incredibly hungover. It had taken me so long to get ready in the morning that there was absolutely no one anywhere in the shipyard to direct me where to go and how to exit. As my friends were waiting for me at the exit, by customs, I went out via the entrance and was completely lost. I eventually made my way back to the group, and we continued on to the home of our Raimo who lived in Helsinki. The son of our friend made us boiled potatoes for breakfast, and a couple of the guys headed into town to the dealership so that they could have a mechanic look at a braking problem on one of the bikes. Apparently they ran into a very famous band in Finland and western Russia called the Leningrad Cowboys. They gave my friends the inside scoop on where to go when we went to Leningrad.

We headed out that day to this summer cottage of our friend's wife. The next day we took a long ride and ended up in Lampinranta, Finland, at this summer cottage of our friend. It was a beautiful ride! At his summer cottage, we spent the evening in the sauna drinking champagne and whiskey and then wading into the lake until about three o'clock in the morning. I will never forget being chest deep in the lake water at one o'clock in the morning just as the sun was setting. We were all able to obtain visas to get into Russia, but they would not allow our capitalistic Harley-Davidsons into their country. Remember, this was before the Iron Curtain came down. We rented a red Honda car and as soon as we got to the Russian border, we were followed by the KGB for the entire rest of our trip. On the ride through the country toward Leningrad, I noticed many people wandering in the woods. I asked our friend what they were doing, and he replied that they were looking for food—actually, yesterday's supper! We were all starting to see and understand how poor this country really was. As soon as we got to our American hotel, we were immediately surrounded by hookers. We told them to go away, and we rented a taxi bus to take us on a tour around town. As a side benefit, the taxi driver was in the black market, and he exchanged our dollars for rubles at a rate of thirteen to one, basically making us very rich by Russian standards. We partied the night away in Russia as bourgeoisie capitalists! We hit every underground bar and discotheque that Leningrad had to offer, for the right amount of money.

As we were trying to get out of town the next morning, we got our directions a little mixed up and had to make a U-turn on one of the horribly decrepit streets in Leningrad. We were immediately pulled over by a Soviet policeman and demanded to show our papers. We were told that the U-turn we made was illegal. We had all decided beforehand that we would try to bribe him and so we did—we gave him fifty bucks and he let us go. In fact, he told us that to get where we wanted to go, we needed to make a U-turn and head in the opposite direction! He and everyone in the car started laughing hysterically.

From Helsinki, we headed over to Stockholm on the ferryboat. On the overnight cruise, we had a few drinks and headed to our tiny four-bed bunk room. Somehow we got on the subject of the funny noises women make while making love. We started laughing uncontrollably as each guy came up with funny names to go along with the noise that was being impersonated. A few examples include Yes Yes Julie, and she would scream, "Yes, yes, yes, yes, yes, *yeeeesssss!*" The Stump Puller would yell, "Umph, argh, argh, eeerrr, yumph, *wuuuuffff!*" California Pinwheel made sounds like someone on an amusement-park ride: "Whoa, yeah, woo-hoo, oh wow, *amaaaazing!*" And then the old Church Girl yelled God's name repeatedly, "Oh God, oh my God, holy God, *ooooh God!*" Those were only a few. We laughed like giddy teenagers for a couple of hours until we all fell asleep. From Stockholm we rode to Oslo, Norway.

The morning we woke up in Oslo, it was pouring rain. We rode from Oslo to the southern tip of the country, along the fjords, in pouring rain. It was rather frightening. The road had many sharp curves, and it wound so close to the drop-off into the water and down the cliffs. When we got to Kristiansand at the southern tip of the country, we were both exhausted and ready to party, and party we did! We went to a knockoff of the bar Hard Rock Cafe. As usual, being four guys with four Harley-Davidsons, we were celebrities. The next morning we took another ferry over to the European mainland and headed to Kassle, Germany. We walked into a bar that evening and they were playing Roy Orbison on the jukebox. I think it was "Pretty Woman." There happened to be a guy sitting at the bar who looked exactly like Roy Orbison! I'm not kidding. We started up a conversation with him, and he showed us around town. It was uneventful, except for me; I tried to buy a hooker with disastrous results. My German wasn't good enough, and I ended up being kicked out of her house before I got my money's worth.

We made our way back to Frankfurt, dropped the motorcycles off, and with a huge sigh of relief were all prepared to head back home. We had one final party at our friend Hans's house. His family owned a vineyard along the Rhine River and on the most beautiful summer evening, without our motorcycles or a worry in the world, we partied with our German friends Hans and Klaus. In our little American group, set aside from the Germans, we talked about our trip. I don't think that I ever have laughed so hard before or since that night.

The group consisted of my district manager friend Fred; a regional sales manager and friend, JC; and a Midwest Harley dealer, Al. It was a fantastic trip, and JC condensed it into a single letter to each of us after we had returned to the USA. Here is what he wrote:

To the band,
Daydreaming is a favorite pastime of mine, and generally those thoughts wander too far off, sometimes to obscure dots on the globe. Living those dreams, however, is truly one of the gifts of life. Working out the plans, getting a group together, and covering all of the details are all parts

of the anticipation that builds the expectations. Seldom in life, however, does the real thing exceed the expectation. When it does, that slice of life should be held up like a crown jewel to be revered and remembered in times that are less fruitful. Such was our journey.

Every time I think of the trip through Europe, I get a smile and an uplift like a shot of adrenaline. When I think back, however, it's not so much what I saw as what I thought, how I felt, and how we experienced those unplanned events.

Remember riding the Rhine and Josef guiding us through the narrow dikes of Holland, coffee shops and window-shopping of Amsterdam, the beer-tasting in Germany, the panic of losing my passport in a foreign country, and oh, Copenhagen from Tivoli to Nyhavn Harbor. Remember the wheat fields and lakes of Sweden, and dinner with Josef and his family. There was a dentist who appeared from nowhere and led us to the ship to Helsinki when we were in Stockholm. If we only had more time there, what a place. What a boat ride. The beautiful harbor islands only led to too much VO whiskey and a free bunk with Al. What more could we have envisioned in Finland? Lakes, countryside, Swiss hospitality, and saunas, male bonding at its finest. Leningrad, nothing more to be said except we are the Leningrad Cowboys and "it's good to be the king." A true friendship was found with Raimo, "Mr. No Problem, I Have a Plan." It actually came by boat, through rain and on to Oslo. Remember the gorgeous ride down the coast on the way to Kristiansand? I remember feeling some fatigue, an overwhelming sense of how truly fortunate we really are, and a torn sensation of being ready to head home but not quite yet. By now, Peter Sellers had been bit by the dog, *das gerschwanzen kaputzen* (okay, we butchered the German language with our weird pig Latin), we had dinner for four in exchange for a leather hat, and the *gerschlittenglazen* was in high season. One more boat trip to Denmark. I'm never going to the can with you guys on a trip again. You ditched me and we wound up in Alborg.

Then the famous Arhus to Kassle Road rally. Al only got us lost once that day, topped off with Fred, "The Jet," taking the lead in grand style on the autobahn. He was just headed for a leisurely weekend in the country, but he wanted to get there at two hundred miles an hour. I've also heard the European circuses are the best, but the one in Kassel was unbelievable. In some ways, we ended up with our friends Klaus and Hans along the Rhine River back in Frankfurt, but in other ways it was just the beginning.

At least for me, the trip made every dimension of the personality expand. I feel broader, deeper, and maybe even a little taller for it. It truly was the adventure of a lifetime, and for that I feel grateful to all of you. I'm reminded of a line from a song on one of those endless cassettes we played: "Ain't that

America," no it certainly ain't. Being back home with the family, safe and sound, was a welcome feeling, yet for days I couldn't concentrate … still full of life from what we had just experienced.

The endless questions of "How was your trip?" put real meaning into the old Harley saying, "For those of you who know, no explanation is necessary, for those of you who don't, no explanation is possible!"

My wife says never again. I have to be true to the code, and if ever I hear the words "We're putting the band back together," I'll be there. Maybe we could call ourselves the Leningrad Cowboys … no, it's already taken.

Abraham Lincoln once said of the pony express, "It was an endeavor of mankind that can only be equaled, never excelled." I think it fits. Together or separately, let's never give up trying to improve on it.

My gratitude to you all,
JC

PS: I've been thinking about a trip from Spain down to Gibraltar, by boat to Africa!

PPS: We could party Casablanca style!!

CHAPTER 9

UNBRIDLED SUCCESS

Everything, except for the purchase of Holiday Rambler, a leading producer of premium quality recreational vehicles, was going well for the corporation and for me individually. I continued to travel from state to state, catching dealers up on the remodeling program. That was in my spare time. The other two parts of my job were overseeing the remodeling blueprints of each and every dealership as it was progressing through the process, and subsequently upon completion of the remodeling to merchandise the store and train the owners and their staff about proper retailing.

After hiring Pam and Shelley and training them, I felt that a great burden would be lifted from my traveling requirements. But the program grew at an exponential rate as the nonparticipating dealers began to see the success of the program. Pam and Shelley began the merchandising in the stores that had finished remodeling. They were now traveling all over the US and doing a fantastic job merchandising and spreading the word as ambassadors of the program to the dealers and the district managers.

Harley-Davidson posted the dealer show in Washington, DC, at the same hotel in which Ronald Reagan had an assassination attempt on him. At the very beginning of the show, there were already problems because we had to deal with unions that worked, as usual, in slow motion if at all. We had to hire security from the union. I showed up an hour and a half early the morning after we had set up our booth and saw the security guard sound asleep in the chair that I had to rent from the union. Some of our merchandise was missing, and many of the hanging signs that only the union could install had not been installed. I went to the union desk to ask for help and was dealt with like I was an idiot. I went into probably the biggest tirade that I have ever delivered in my professional career. I will not go into details, but the unions at that particular venue are by far a stereotypical slander on unions. Well, apparently Clark couldn't sleep that night and went for a walk and was mugged. I have a strong suspicion that he went out for another type of walk and the guy got close to him and stole his wallet. Clark claimed that the guy gave him a hug and he was mugged. The girls came up with this song: "I was walking through the park one day, in the very merry month of July, and what to my surprise, a man with angel eyes, came up to give me a hug and I turned out getting mugged, in the very merry month of July!"

That same dealer show was fairly uneventful—except for the last night. I had a suite at the hotel with my hotel upgrades. I went to bed early like a good guy, knowing that I had a lot of traveling to do for the rest of the month. I had also signed up about twenty more dealers for the remodeling program and needed to do personal visits. Just as I was falling asleep, Pam called me and said, "Boss, please don't shoot the messenger, but there is a party on its way up to your room." Before she could hang up, there was a knock on my door, and when I opened the door, in my boxer shorts, there was a throng of about twenty-five people. Most of them were Harley-Davidson employees, and a few of them were Harley-Davidson dealers and their employees. But there was one woman who came in from the room next door. After we partied all night and they drank every drink from my minibar, the entire crowd left except for her, the girl next door. She was the daughter of a diplomat from South America spending her summer with her father in North America. We had sex that probably lasted until five o'clock in the morning. When she went to get into the shower, I heard an audible shriek when the water hit her sore coochie. When she came out of the shower, she explained that she was glad she didn't live here because if we were a couple and we would have the sex like that, she wouldn't be able to walk anymore.

At about that same time, Harley-Davidson International wanted to develop its own store design program in Europe. They hired a guy who had been nothing more than a motorcycle mechanic. They wanted me to train him. He traveled with me a couple of times and met with Clark Richey. Those without ultimate wisdom decided he was ready to persuade the European dealers to remodel their stores. I knew it was a big mistake and tried to tell my boss and the rest of upper management. My words fell on deaf ears. I had to work with this knucklehead for a couple of years. Also at the same time I was taking over management of the Canadian dealer network and overseeing their appointee for a similar position. He was a tiny little fellow, and what many people would refer to as a nerd. Don't get me wrong, he was a good guy with great intentions, but he had a background in grocery stores. Oh boy. My hands were full, and my mind was about to explode.

I was invited to Banff, Canada, by the Dealy Corporation, which was the sole distributor for Harley-Davidson as well as many other motorcycle manufacturers in Canada. If you've never been to Banff, it is a beautiful place nestled in the mountains near the west coast. I had an excellent show presenting the store design program along with my Canadian counterpart. I was also accompanied by a recently hired intern from Harley-Davidson corporate. Mack was a good guy and strikingly handsome. I had to room with him, as we were the only two Americans from Harley-Davidson invited to the show. He happened to be the liaison from Milwaukee for Canada. We had a great show, and Mack found a Canadian girl and wanted to take her back to our room. I told him I would give him an hour and a half and then come knocking on the door. After an hour and a half sleeping in the car in the parking lot, I went back to the room and could hear him still pleading to get some action. I knocked on the door anyway, and he asked me to give him another half hour. I walked across the street where there was a natural sulfur pool. I climbed over the fence and spent another hour smoking a cigar in the evening in the pool under the fantastic and clear

Canadian night sky. I went back to the room and Mack had still not closed the deal. I told her she had to go and that was that.

My next dealer show in Canada was in Halifax. That was a great town, and the people were wonderful. Everywhere I went it seemed as if they had been smoking marijuana, because they were in such a great mood. At the initial evening dinner and cocktail party, a tall dark-haired woman with blue eyes approached me as if she had known me for years. She claimed she had met me and knew me from the dealer shows in the US. She was a vendor for the Canadian dealer network, and for the life of me I don't know what she sold. All I can tell you is that she was selling sex to me, except for free. For the next three straight days—early in the morning, during lunch breaks, and all night long—all we did was have sex. It was not only great, but incredible. She was a screamer, and I'm sure everyone in the hotel knew exactly what was going on. She wasn't married and neither was I, so I actually saw a glimmer of potential. Yeah, right.

A few of us traveled to Frankfurt to merchandise the first couple stores in Europe that had been remodeled under the program. One of our destinations was the dealership in Berlin. After a wild night on the town, on motorcycles, we managed, separately, to make our way back to the hotel. We all woke up with extreme hangovers, and one guy was just begging me for some aspirin. I instructed him to go into my shaving kit and take the white pills that were marked aspirin. I made sure to mention that because I had pills that looked very similar to aspirin but were 1000 mg of niacin that I was taking as a natural preventative to cholesterol. If you know anything about niacin, even 50 mg will make you feel like you are on fire. Of course, he took the wrong pills, and to exacerbate the hangover, he had taken 2000 mg of niacin and basically went insane. After eight hours of hard work in what Europe calls an air-conditioned store, he was feeling better, and we borrowed a couple of motorcycles and went to the newly torn-down Berlin Wall. I chipped a couple of dozen pieces, but this guy was on a mission. He spent two more hours than I did going from spot to spot trying to chip just the right piece that suited him. He was finally nearly driving me insane. I knew there was no way I could work with this guy.

I traveled up to Calgary, Canada, to help work with the dealership there on its remodeling project. Calgary is known as the northern Texas. They have a lot of cowboys up there, and they love to chew tobacco. The dealers were no exception. Also, as dealers, the first stop they wanted to make was to take me to a strip club. The strip clubs in Canada are the best. The girls are totally nude. One guy wasn't used to this, and he acted just like a twelve-year-old seeing his first naked girl. The two dealers and I had taken a pinch of chew tobacco and put it between her cheek and gum. This kid asked for some also. We were drinking beers by the bucket. Within about five minutes he asked for some more chew. We looked at him and the three of us knew what was happening. He had swallowed the chew while drinking his beer. It was only a matter of minutes. I wouldn't have given him more tobacco but they, as an evil gesture, gave him another pinch. Within about five more minutes, he bolted from his chair, and we found him later in the women's restroom, lying in a stall after puking all night long. He was a sissy. I don't know what it is about guys who think that they can hang with me and do this stuff that I can do and do it the way that I do it. I grew up with the best. My brother Jimmy and my best friend Rick taught me everything I know about drinking and women and life. And after you get a little bit of knowledge, you start to understand who to trust, what to look for, and what to believe in.

I was in York, Pennsylvania, at the Harley-Davidson final assembly plant where I had been invited to give a detailed presentation to the sales department on the subject of the store remodeling program. I was staying at the Holiday Inn in York along with all the district sales managers. My longtime friend and fellow district manager Hal had left the company and bought a dealership in San Antonio, Texas. My other district manager friend Marti had been let go by David for inappropriate use of his expense account. One of the only other district managers who I really enjoyed hanging out with was David from California. He came to work for Harley-Davidson from the brake manufacturer Kelsey-Hayes. We actually left the bar uncharacteristically before midnight. As we were heading back toward separate rooms, we passed the room of several rookie district managers still working on their initial orders for their dealers' motorcycle shipments for the beginning of the new model year. David and I went into their room just to hassle them little bit because they were the new guys. David started pulling all of the pillows and blankets off of the beds and throwing them around the room. He then flipped the mattress onto the floor, turned the box spring on its side, and threw it up against the wall. As you know, on the bottom of box springs there is usually a thin fiber material that resembles Fiberglas. There was a small hole and for some reason, I whipped out my manhood and stuck it in the hole as I was telling the new guys to go screw themselves, just like this. At that same moment, David grabbed a corner of the fiber sheeting and ripped it off the bottom of the box spring, with my penis still inside the hole. It scratched me pretty badly, and I went into the bathroom to examine the damage and to stop the bleeding. I came out with my dick wrapped in toilet paper that was now soaked in blood. We all got a big laugh out of it. The only person who didn't think it was funny was my boss, who tried to get me fired. He didn't even know the whole story, but he called me into Human Resources telling them that I had purposely taken a knife and cut my own penis in front of the group. After I threatened them with legal action, Human Resources dropped the issue and the boss-man walked away with his tail between his legs. David later went on to buy a dealership with Wayne, the Pencil Neck, out west.

I went to visit David just before he left the company. I was with one of my employees, Pam. When we got to the airport on our way to San Diego, we went to the ticket counter and were informed that our flight was preparing to depart and that we had to hurry through security with no time to check our bags. I always checked my bags because I carried a small .38 caliber handgun and ammunition. I always kept them separate, and it is legal to ship your bags that way. When I got to security, I informed them that I had a gun. The senior citizen who was handling the X-ray machine pushed an alarm bell, and airport security and police descended upon Pam and me like ants. After showing them all of my necessary identification and explaining the situation, he tried to look in their computer system to see if I was wanted by the police. The police department computer system was not working at that time, specifically their airport computer system. They had no other choice but to arrest me and take me to jail. Pam was beside herself and didn't know what to do. She faithfully delayed her flight and took a taxi to the police station to bail me out. During the processing at the police station, one of the officers found out that I worked for Harley-Davidson and told me that he would get me out of there within the hour. The federal government dropped all charges, but the district attorney for the city was a bitch. She insisted on pursuing concealed gun charges against me. After a couple thousand dollars in legal fees, we agreed on ninety days state court probation and time served.

CHAPTER 10

A BIKE TRIP THROUGH EUROPE WITH MY BUDDY

THE TRIP STARTED AS a pipe dream at about midnight on a beautiful summer evening in 1989, after Jim and I had been drinking all night at the Pacific Beach Bar in San Diego where they were playing some great live rhythm and blues. Jim, who was in outstanding guitar player, always took me to the local oceanfront bars that had fantastic live music playing. Being an excellent musician, he had a knack for finding little hole-in-the-wall taverns where up-and-coming musicians would play. Actually, we started talking about it before that at a Moody Blues concert that was held in San Diego. What on earth could be more exciting than discussing and planning a motorcycle trip through Europe on Harley-Davidsons with one of your lifelong best friends? The answer is obvious: nothing!

It took about a year, but Jim and I committed to a time frame that would work for both of us, as he was still working in the insurance industry and needed to plan far ahead. We talked every week about where we wanted to go and what we needed to bring. We thought about, and dreamed about, and talked about every possible combination of events that a couple of single guys could imagine while planning a trip of a lifetime. Jim and I had had a lot of escapades in a lot of bars with a lot of women all over the country, but we were both certain that this would be the coup de grâce of any adventure that we'd ever had together. We had played football together, and even before that, we had ridden our minibikes together. We were roommates together while he finished college.

Planning a trip with friends brings back memories of the friendships you have held so close to your heart, because you can envision a continuation of the wonderful feelings you've always had during those special times with your friends. I'd known Jim's parents since I was in about eighth grade. You get to know a lot about a person after you live with him for a while, and you see the type of people who come in and out of his life. When Jim and I lived together, he had a 1979 Harley-Davidson Roadster and I had a 1970 triumph 650 Tiger. Jim and I did a lot of riding in those days, and we picked up a lot of girls.

My favorite memory of our time together in our bachelor pad was shortly after Jim graduated. He'd parted on a monthlong trip in a camper he borrowed from his brother through the south of the United States. When he came home, I asked him how many girls he had met, and he said none. I told him I was going to take him to a place where we could both get laid, and we went to a small bar on the south side of Milwaukee called Willie's. We walked in, picked up two girls, came home, and got laid. Another time, shortly after that, Jim and I went out separately and returned to the apartment. We both had met women, and after having sex with them, we both apparently took a break at the same time. As our bedroom doors opened, the women came out and knew each other, calling out each other's names and hugging. Is that what they mean by a small world?

Anyway, we continued to plan the trip, and with every telephone conversation laughed and joked about our past lives and how great this trip would be. That just happens to be part of the fun of planning a trip with a true friend. We settled on October 3, 1990, for a start date. It was difficult to coordinate the logistics of meeting on the East Coast at the same time as I was traveling from Milwaukee in the Midwest and Jim was traveling from Southern California. It didn't work out perfectly—in fact it kind of got very screwed up. After a nightmare of trying to figure out where each of us was, before the days of cell phones, we finally found each other. I was upstairs and he was downstairs at the same gate. When we got on the flight, the stewardess told us that the booze was free on international flights. We partied and convinced all the stewardesses that we were members of the Harley International Race Team. And so we found ourselves on the evening flight from Boston to Frankfurt.

Jim and I took a taxi from the Frankfurt airport for GmbH, where our motorcycles were waiting for us. Interesting for me to see that times had changed and security at the airport was now made up of military men carrying automatic weapons in what appeared to be a ready-to-shoot posture.

Jim had spent a semester during college in Europe and wanted to relive part of that trip by spending our first night in a youth hostel. I was not a fan of the idea, but I figured that I would do this for my buddy. We headed out south of Frankfurt and stopped in the little town where Jim had made arrangements for us to stay at the youth hostel. I had no idea what to expect, and my worst fears were about to come true. By definition, they were all young people, and I mean less than sixteen years old. We got a room bunking with a group of four teenagers! Jim and I claimed our bunks and went out on the town for the rest of the night and partied. When we got back, all the teenagers were drunk, and if it weren't for my innate parental control, they would have been out of control all evening. I do have a fond memory of Jim sitting on the windowsill writing in his diary about the day's events. It seemed a little odd to me, seeing his silhouette against the sunny window, in a crouching position, writing in his diary like a young boy would do. There was a part of me that felt jealous that I never took the time to write down anything about my life. Jim always felt it was important to document his life with photographs and diaries about the things he had done in the places he had been. Later in my life, I admired that more and more. Jim truly was a great friend.

The next morning we headed toward France. The town we ended up in was Strasbourg. We found a hotel along the river, checked in, and went for a long run along the river for about an hour. Jim was always a good workout buddy, and we both loved to run. In fact, every time Jim and I got together, no matter where we were—

Milwaukee, San Diego, the dealer shows—we always put on our running gear and headed out to anyplace that was flat and straight. Jim and I used to run around the San Diego State University track. After a major remodeling of the track and football field, I had an evil idea to cut up a large area of the Astroturf and put it in Jim's front and back yard. Even though he liked the idea, he talked me out of it.

Leaving France—and by the way, fuck the French—we headed over to Munich. We went from hotel to hotel and could not find a room, so we kept heading south, stopping at every *Zimmer Frei* (room for rent). They were all full. The last place we stopped, the woman gave me directions to a hotel in the middle of nowhere, south of Munich. It was late at night, and both of our gas tanks were nearly on empty. We pulled into the hotel and parked our motorcycles. We walked in behind an older couple and eventually checked in. As it so happened, as we made our way to our room, it was right next to the people who were checking in before us. We were pretty tired and just wanted to go to sleep. Within five minutes, our lights were out ... but within one minute more, we started to hear the couple next door making noises. It's part of the funny noises that women make while making love—all we heard was, "uf da ... uuf daa, uuuf daaa, uuuuf daaaa, uuuuuuuuf daaaaaaaaaaaaaaaaaaaaaaaaaaaaaa aaaa!" A German Stump Puller. That was exactly what we heard, and Jim and I have laughed about that for the past twenty years!

We took our time riding through the Black Forest, which is absolutely breathtaking, especially on a motorcycle. We went across the border and into Switzerland and found a hotel in Zurich that was in the middle of all the activity one would want to experience. We spent the night walking through the town, and the next morning—as unusual as it may seem—Jim and I went window-shopping around the jewelry district of Zurich. The only place we entered was a watch shop that sold Rolex watches. After a lot of deliberation and negotiation, I bought my first Rolex for about US$800. I have had that watch ever since, and have only had to send it back to the manufacturer for cleaning and maintenance. After the purchase, the gentleman who sold me the Rolex asked me if I wanted to pay the tax with the purchase. I said no. He explained that if I took the watch over the border, the authorities would probably ask me for a receipt. Being very naïve, I explained that I would simply wear the watch. In his broken English and German accent, he said, "You go to the border, and they will find the box. When they find the coffin, they will ask, where is the body?" The very thought of that and how he said it has stayed with me for my entire life as a lesson to never try to lie to government officials.

Munich to Zurich was beautiful, but mark my words: the ride from Zurich, Switzerland, to Innsbruck, Austria, cannot be matched by any ride that I have ever taken in my entire life. Jim and I took roads up through the mountains and over the pass, and when we finally arrived in Innsbruck, the town that greeted us was almost beyond our ability to comprehend. Jim and I checked into a tiny little hotel that had a Chinese restaurant on the first floor, so we had Chinese food that night in Austria. All I remember about that night was that in Europe, they don't have screens on the windows, and it was hot and the mosquitoes were out so we woke up in the morning with a lot of mosquito bites. In the morning, we took a jog all the way up to the castle, probably one of the toughest workouts I have ever had. Along the way, Jim and I passed a small enclosed pool area that must have been the equivalent of a trailer park in the US, and we couldn't help but notice the women sunbathing without their tops. What is it that makes a man want to stare at a woman's boobs? Anyway, with all our mosquito bites, Jim and I toured Innsbruck and the next day headed north back into Germany and toward Frankfurt.

We made our way safely into Frankfurt and arrived at GmbH to drop off the motorcycles that they had so graciously afforded us. While we were dropping off the motorcycles, I met a young woman who worked there by the name of Ella. I struck up a conversation with her, invited her out for dinner, and asked if she had a friend who could accompany her for my friend, Jim. She said she had a single roommate, and we planned to get together that night.

Now you have to remember that my German is not very good, and so I'm not sure that my translation of asking her to ask her friend to come with us was accurate, but I had faith! Well, after we had dropped off the motorcycles, the girls came to meet us and we spent the next two days touring Frankfurt. I think the highlight of the tour was in the Frankfurt train station, where some German guy, high on ecstasy, came over and tried to slap Ella. I immediately jumped up to defend her, but she was quicker than I and defended herself, sending that crazy man away. Ella and I could have been a couple, I have no doubt, but it was not to be. Jim and her roommate had nothing in common. Ella and I slept together that night, and the next morning she graciously took Jim and me to the airport.

We flew back into Boston, and when we got there after an uneventful flight, Jim and I hugged each other like the brothers we were before going to different terminals and different planes to two different places, with a deep feeling that we now knew each other much more than most people will ever tell—trusting and knowing that we had a deeper relationship than most people will ever have. Motorcycle trips can take you to places you never knew existed. After twenty years of knowing each other, we knew each other better.

If there is any way to build a relationship for life with a friend, there is nothing better than going on a motorcycle trip, no matter where it is. We flew back to separate places, but had each other forever in our hearts. Within the next year, I recommended my buddy for a district manager position in California. He got the job and is still the DM there today.

CHAPTER 11

ALL THE WAY TO TANGIERS

In the fall of 1991, the Leningrad Cowboys minus Al planned and executed another trip to Europe. This particular motorcycle trip was going to be a very interesting and exciting adventure. The new group of JC, Fred, Johnny, and I were going to fly to Paris and travel through southern Europe for one week and then have our significant others fly into Madrid for one week. We would then travel through southern Spain and Portugal, over to Tangiers, and then the women would fly home and us guys would continue north back to Paris. As I was the only guy in the group who did not have a significant other at the time, I invited my sister Gini. Everyone was greatly anticipating the trip.

We ordered a minivan taxi to pick us all up at the Harley-Davidson headquarters on Juneau Avenue. I think it was JC who clambered into the van with a bottle of champagne to celebrate the beginning of our trip. As an experienced air traveler, I normally never drank before or during a flight. We drank the champagne all the way to the airport, continued to drink at the airport, and I had a few drinks on the plane. The flight to Europe was an overnight flight, and even with all the drinking I barely got an hour's sleep. When we arrived in Paris, not only was I hungover, but I'd had very little sleep. I really felt like shit.

We took a taxi from Charles de Gaulle airport to the main Harley-Davidson dealership in Paris. This is where we picked up our motorcycles. We were all pretty exhausted but decided, as a group, to tour Paris all in one day. We hit every one of the tourist sites in Paris in one day, including three guys going up to the top of the Eiffel Tower. I have a fear of heights, so I made it to about the eighth floor and decided that I would be better off—and they would be better off—without me. I went down and lay on the grass and took a nap while they enjoyed the beautiful view from the top of the tower.

The next day, we all headed down to Monaco. The Harley-Davidson dealer incentive award trip was going to be held at the Hotel Monaco later in the year. We had made arrangements with our travel department at Harley corporate to get two rooms complimentary, acting as forward scouts for the group of five hundred Harley-Davidson people who would be coming later in the year. Pulling up on our motorcycles and being from Harley-Davidson corporate, we were immediately treated like celebrities. As usual, we were allowed to park our motorcycles directly in front of the hotel as if they were Rolls-Royces or Maseratis or Jaguars. For the next three days, we were treated as kings, all complimentary.

We took our time and followed a fairly direct route

to Madrid. This is where we were going to pick up the rest of our party, which included the other guys' wives and my sister Gini. As seasoned travelers, we were all completely aware of how jet-lagged they would be. We planned to make the first day for them as short as possible on the motorcycles and headed directly to the Costa del Sol. We stopped at a little restaurant along the way in the middle of nowhere just to have a bite of lunch. We were kind of in the middle of nowhere, somewhere in the eastern part of Spain, and the restaurant had chickens and cows surrounding it. Funny enough, my sister wasn't feeling well from the airplane trip, as she also suffers from claustrophobia, so she ordered only chicken soup. The menu said it was fresh. When they brought her bowl of chicken soup out, it actually had a chicken feather in it! With true style and grace, she picked out the chicken feather and ate the soup.

After we were done with lunch, my sister asked me if I knew where the bathroom was. Before I gave her directions, I explained to her that she was only going to find a hole in the ground and perhaps a rag or a hose with which to clean herself off. She gave me one of those looks of incredulity that only an older sister can give her younger brother. Within thirty seconds, she came running back out of the bathroom telling me that there was only a hole to urinate in! I said, "I told you! Just pull out of your pants, put your feet where the foot marks are, squat down, and urinate." On the rest of the ride that afternoon to the eastern coast of Spain, that was all she could talk about while she was sitting on the back of the motorcycle screaming into my ear. We had a beautiful and leisurely ride all the way to Valencia. That night, we walked into town and had a marvelous meal of paella. I was so happy. I was with my sister and everyone was happy, and it felt like heaven.

The next day we took a long ride all around the southeastern coast of Spain to Gibraltar. The following morning we were going to take a ferryboat to Tangiers, Africa. We arrived in Gibraltar late in the afternoon and made reservations for dinner in our hotel, which happened to have a live flamenco-dancing group performing that evening. We were given a table adjacent to the dance floor, and Gini and I sat at the seats closest to the performers. As we were eating our meal, the performers began to dance. The main performer looked exactly like a rat! He would come within inches of my sister and me as he was tapping out his flamenco dance. I knew what was going to happen next. My sister could not help but notice the similarity between this guy and a rat. Every time he got close, she would tap me on the shoulder and say, "Bowzer, look at that guy, he looks just like a rat." I was laughing so hard inside, but I was also trying not to be rude in front of the performer. I felt like I was going to explode. I finally had to turn around and tell her to shut up. It was hilarious!

We took the ferryboat to Tangiers and passed the Rock of Gibraltar on our way. Even on those short rides, I still got seasick. Everybody was making fun of me, with beers in hand, swinging back and forth. After we got off the ferryboat and headed to the customs interrogation point, we found that all of our research was correct in that the officials wanted a bribe. They told us that our insurance papers were not in order and that we needed to purchase more insurance for the motorcycles to be in the back country. We argued for five minutes and realized that our bantering was to no avail. We paid the money and went on our way. We checked into the hotel that Forbes stayed at with his Harley-Davidson motorcycle.

That night in Tangiers was actually quite magical. We were informed by the hotel management that we should hire security to guard our motorcycles overnight. They recommended a guy, and we paid him in advance—and of course, he was not there in the morning. Nothing special happened, but it was truly an amazing city. The roadways were not roadways but pathways instead, only five feet wide. We ate the local cuisine and did a walking tour of the city. The next morning JC wanted to buy a carpet and have it shipped to his house. We found a little merchant and had to walk up through three or four flights looking through carpets until JC and Marci found the perfect one. Now it starts to get a little weird. These merchants did not want to let us leave until JC and Marci purchased that carpet! It was getting more and more intense, and I finally said that I was taking my sister and leaving. Since I was the biggest guy in the room by far, I had little resistance. Fortunately, that was enough of an opening to get the whole group out of the building.

We left and continued to walk around the city, and at one point my sister decided to take a picture of some bearded old man selling small trinkets on the curb. As soon as she took his picture, he came running after her trying to get the camera from her, and she came screaming to me, "Bowzer, Bowzer, help me!" I stood in front of a guy and he backed off, yelling something in his foreign language. I'm pretty sure that it was something like "Fuck you!"

After a day of shopping in Tangiers, we packed our motorcycles with our belongings and prepared to head back to Spain and on to Portugal. The entire time we were there, a throng of locals were just waiting to sell us the trinkets that they had inside their coats. Speaking in wild tongues, they converged on Gini as well as the rest of us and were too close for comfort. For safety reasons, I was carrying my sister's money, so even though I was preparing the motorcycle for takeoff, she was tugging on my leather jacket and saying, "Bowzer, Bowzer, gimme some money, I want to buy some of this stuff!" I was just trying to get the hell out of there. I gave her some money and she bought some crap, and we got the hell out of Tangiers.

We rode all the way to Seville after getting off the ferryboat. We spent the night near Coimbra in Portugal. It was a typical, wonderful summer evening in a strange and foreign town. We had dinner outdoors and retired into the bar that had bottles of libation we'd never seen before. The group, except for my sister and I, wanted to—and did—try every unusual drink that was on the bar shelf. Gini and I decided to go to sleep early. I knew the morning would come early and that we had a long day to ride. Thank God, because the next day turned out to be hell.

It was about 125 degrees all the way from our last destination to dropping the women off in Madrid, and we had miscalculated the distance and the time it would take to travel that far. As we were riding, I was last in the line of four motorcycles. Something was splashing on my windshield and I couldn't tell what it was. I stood up on my foot pegs and was splashed in the face with more fluid. I thought perhaps one of my friends had been opening a water bottle that, by the Venturi effect, was pulling water out and splashing it all over me. As I sped up while complaining to my sister, I realized that it was Fred's wife puking! Her puke was splashing me in the face and splashing my motorcycle. Lovely.

The ride to Madrid is one of the longest and hottest rides I've ever taken, except for a ride going through the Mojave Desert that nearly killed me. We dropped the girls off at the Madrid airport but went inside because I wanted to write my first and only Dear Jane letter to this girl Lacey I had been dating. I basically told her that it was over and asked my sister to mail it when she got back to the USA.

After leaving the women off, we decided to watch a major bullfight. We bought some wine and whiskey and a few sandwiches and had a picnic prior to the bullfight. The bullfight was probably the most horrible event I have ever witnessed in my life. I guess I was naïve, but I never really thought that they actually kill the bull. It was the most bloody and least courageous sporting event I have ever witnessed. After it was over, as we walked out in a crowd of about 25,000 people, all of a sudden, from behind, here comes Johnny's wife and Fred's wife! Their flight had been canceled and rescheduled for the next morning, and the airline got them a taxi. They brought along a friend they'd met, also stranded, a pretty good-looking girl from Chicago. I ended up have sex with her early that evening. She was tall and thin, almost as tall as me.

When JC and I went to our hotel, it just so happened

that the winning bullfighter was staying there. The hotel had a buffet of different local foods, and I think it was happy hour so we could get two drinks for one. This bullfighter looked like he was sixteen years old. We talked with him a lot and Fred gave him a whole bunch of Harley trinkets. I convinced JC to follow me to a whorehouse that we had passed on the way into town. We should never have ridden our bikes, because we were pretty drunk. When we walked into this place, which was a dump, we both knew we had made a mistake. Some ugly little toothless girl came up to JC and said, "Fucky fucky, sucky sucky?" JC immediately took her hand and put it on my crotch and said, "Ask him!" We scrambled out of there as fast as we could. Glad I had JC as security.

The next morning, we headed up into southern France and traveled through, and spent two nights in the Cognac and Bordeaux regions on our way to Paris to return our motorcycles and spend two days relaxing after such a long ride. As soon as we left Madrid, I knew something was wrong. I had a horrible pain in my back around my kidneys. The pain was excruciating. I was barely able to keep up with the group; I had to continually pull over because I had diarrhea. It was hot, I was sweating, we were trying to make time, and being bullheaded I tried to stick with the group. That's just what to do. That leg to Paris was very difficult for me because of the physical pain and the actual need to stop every half hour and either urinate or crap. We went through a small French town and I stopped at a pharmacy. Using my English-to-French translation book, I told the pharmacist that I had very bad back pain and painful diarrhea. They acted as if they didn't know what I was talking about. I showed them the translation in the book and they continued to act as if they had no idea what I was talking about. I finally pointed at my ass and made the sound of a huge fart! They all began laughing and handed me a box of pills, charged me, and sent me on my way. By the way, the pills ended up being of no value.

In Paris we had a wonderful hotel, but I really wasn't in the mood to enjoy any part of the next two days. We had dropped the Harley-Davidsons off at the local dealership in Paris, and while we were there we met a great guy who owned a very exclusive club of Harley-Davidson riders. He invited us to tour the city with him as his guests. We were all excited, but there was no way I could do it. I was just too sick. JC, Johnny, and Fred went with this guy, by limousine, and toured Paris in style—Harley style! I missed it, but that was okay because I really didn't feel well at all. It was a long two days I spent lying in bed. We flew home the next day, uneventfully. I'm sorry I missed the tour around Paris because from what the guys told me, it was incredible and a once-in-a-lifetime experience. Then again, there was a part of me that didn't care because I was too sick to give a damn.

CHAPTER 12

GLASS HOUSES

IN 1991, WE HAD a dealer show in Orlando, Florida, at the Disney World Dolphin Hotel. After the first night cocktail party, I walked into the main bar where I knew all my friends would be. I was immediately attracted to a woman sitting with another couple at a table in the bar. As I was talking to my friend who was the district manager for those particular dealers, he informed me that she was the daughter, or actually the granddaughter, of the dealers in Seaford, Delaware. I couldn't help myself. I walked right up to the table and, unfortunately, scared her as I tried to introduce myself. That should have been a sign. Theresa and I fell in love within moments of my talking to her. She was there with her mom and stepfather, Gail and Bob. We talked for the rest of the night and ended up making love in the fire escape at the Dolphin Hotel. We were right outside her parents' room. For the next three nights, we spent as much time as we could together. I invited her over to Pleasure Island at Disney World, and she showed up wearing the most beautiful dress I had ever seen on a woman in my entire life. It was a black spandex tight-fitting miniskirt, and she looked fantastic. She had big boobs and big hips and a tiny waist. I would later find out that they were manufactured by plastic surgeons. We made love every time we could; even near the tennis courts, being bitten by mosquitoes. For the first time in my life, I really thought that I had found a woman that I could marry. Wow … even though I went through my whole life wanting to be single, I was wrong—and boy, was I wrong. The last night we were together I had specifically designed to take several hours to tell each other our entire history from birth. To my surprise, she told me about family issues since the time she could remember. For some reason, the White Knight syndrome kicked into effect, and I was prepared to do anything and everything to take care of this woman. Even though we vowed to meet again after the dealer show, we only got together a couple of times. I invited her on my trip to Barbados that was coming up in a couple of months.

My boss had been changing into more and more of an intolerable bureaucrat. He had gone from being the best boss I ever had to being maniacal. We shared a secretary, because his boss was so cheap. He was starting to nitpick everything I did and never mentioned the incredible success that the program had under my direction. He brought me into his office once and proclaimed that a dealer from California complained that he had witnessed me watching a girl take her top off and sit on my motorcycle. The conversation was pretty simple. I said "And so what?"

And he said in his omnipotent manner, "Well, what would you have done if Rich Teerlink was there?"

I responded that I would've done the same damn thing! I am single, and I like tits. This dealer turned out to be a sneaky little shit just like I thought he was. He was a short little piece of crap. No one liked him. But I will tell you that he is a grown-up tattletale.

The secretary my boss and I shared, Toni, was a very pretty woman and a very competent employee. She kept up with all of my administrative needs, and I assumed that she did the same for my boss, Chuck. Or, wait … during his tenure, Chuck had changed his name to Charles and his wife had changed her name from Deb to Debra. Apparently, they got some information somewhere that in order for Chuck to be promoted to a VP, he and his wife would have to have more formal names. While this was going on, Toni had come to me in private and confided that someone in the company had been sexually harassing her (I witnessed this). Not only had he been doing it in person, but he had been tormenting her by leaving her messages of explicit sexual desires on his dictation tapes. After I learned about this, and after attending multiple sexual-harassment seminars, I knew it was my obligation to go to the vice president of HR and discuss with him the information I had. He initially thought I was referring to one of the upper executives. Then again, the vice president of Human Resources also seemed a little odd to me.

On the district manager trip to Barbados, I took Theresa. On the first night, on the balcony overlooking the courtyard of our resort complex, as well as a dozen people in a hot tub, I got on one knee and asked her to marry me. She accepted. One of the people in the hot tub was Clark Richey. He walked up under the balcony in his bathrobe and asked us in his unusual voice, "Is it true?" It sounded like he was sad. I told him yes, that we were engaged, and he turned on his heel. As he walked away, he exclaimed, "I will send champagne." At any rate, shortly after the trip to Barbados for all the district managers, my current boss left the building forever. *Good riddance* was my thought.

With the good comes the bad. Now I would report directly to one of the upper executives. It seemed to me that this upper executive disliked anyone who wasn't a woman. I thought that he was a very disrespectful man. For the short time that I reported directly to him, I found it almost unbearable to go into meetings with him. He was so disrespectful that he would take his shoes off and put his feet on his desk with his socked feet pointing directly at me, and he would open his shirt and massage his breast while talking to me. I thought that he was a disgusting little mother's boy. At least my boss was gone, and a great burden was lifted from the organization, because he was an employee who didn't fit. He had a beautiful wife who adored him and a wonderful child who had just entered high school. I never did like the way he talked about women. It gave me a creepy feeling. That's exactly how he made me feel. Harley-Davidson had fired several men for sexual harassment. The higher up they were in the company, different terms were used for their departure. That's unfortunate, because they could cover up a predator who would go on to the next job and do the same thing. Harley-Davidson released a man from Human Resources who I thought was kind of a pathetic guy. To the corporation, he was a standup Human Resource professional. Whenever I had lunch with him, the only thing he had to say were racial jokes and personal slanders about other employees. I guess that was his way of trying to bond with a guy like me. It only disgusted me and made me loathe upper management that much more for their hypocrisy.

At this time, I had taken my remodeling endeavors to Asia. Our Asian wholly owned subsidiary was Harley-Davidson of Japan. I was engaged and now responsible for all the dealerships worldwide. After several despicable incidents with my coworker who was going through a divorce, we decided that it was time the Motor Company severed its relationship with his employment. He begged and cried, but we finally were able to convince Human Resources to let him go. He was another piece of cancer cut out of the organization that I had become completely and undeniably a member of. I had finally come to the point where I realized how much I loved Harley-Davidson Motor Company, even with all its faults.

Benefits of being the owner of
Milwaukee Harley-Davidson.

10 year employment award.

Boiler room preperation. Jam those bikes!

*Unused 100th Anniversary tickets to all
the events around the world.*

Willie G and I at the opening of the new building.

Team Harley (from left) Hal, my brother Eddie,
Gerry and Rick. Cannonball One Lap of America

Front cover Dealernews magazine

Point of Purchase Advertising International award.

My sister Gini and I on the ferry to Tangiers.
Rock of Gebraltor in the background.

My first Company Owned Vehical plate at Harley.

My buddy Jim and I in Germany.

Jim and I in Yosemite 15 years after our Europe trip.

GmbH in the mid 1980s.

Wooden train whistle I received for giving a speech at the 50th Anniversary of the engine plant.

100th Anniversary gold & silver key.

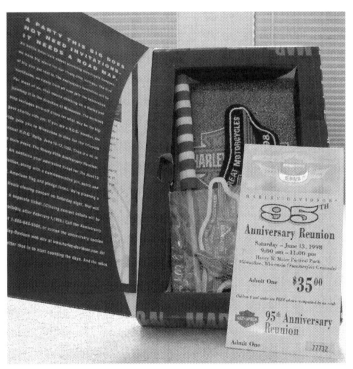

Original 95th Anniversary ticket packet.

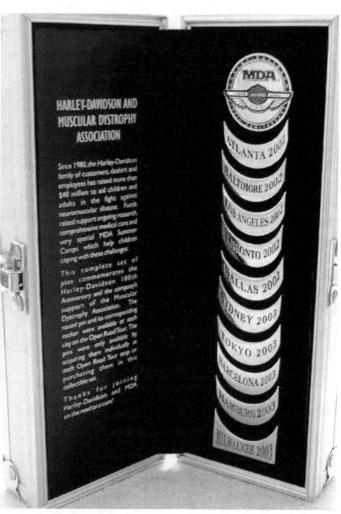

Cities that hosted the 100th Anniversary flop events.

In 1991 Harley was basically capable of
only producing black painted bikes.

Jaguar presented this to me after a speech
I gave to their top 50 U.S. dealers.

Limited Edition pins from 50th - 100th Anniversary.

Maggie & Tony on their wedding day.

My first Dealer Show in Nashville.

Planning and hard work during the 95th paved
the way to a successful 100th Anniversary.

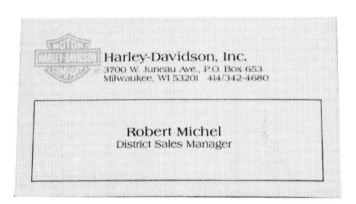

The magic business card.

Top 10 dealer Pegasus award for retailing Buells.

Robert S. (Bob) Michel 2013.

CHAPTER 13

MY HARLEYMOON

THERESA AND I WERE married on Father's Day of 1992. It was a simple church wedding in a white chapel Lutheran church. We had about a hundred guests, and poor Theresa was shaking like a terrified bird during the entire ceremony. My nephew Nick played the violin, and my niece Erica sang a love song. We had a wedding reception at the Hubbard Park Lodge in Shorewood, Wisconsin. It is a stunningly beautiful old log cabin building adjacent to the Milwaukee River. I actually planned the entire wedding and reception, including the food and decorations.

Everyone we invited actually attended, and we had a great time celebrating our marriage. I drank way too much and fell asleep on the living-room floor, partially because I knew I had to work the next day and be there at eight a.m. Theresa and I both went to work the next day, and I had a very important meeting with the vice president, Jim Patterson. He was shocked that I actually showed up for the meeting the day after my wedding. But through a confluence of circumstances, leaving for our honeymoon on Tuesday was actually best for us both, schedule-wise and financially.

We flew into Frankfurt and picked up our motorcycle at GmbH. The first day, we rode the motorcycle for about one hour and stayed at a beautiful hotel overlooking the Rhine River. The hotel was really a renovated castle that was about five hundred years old. All we did was have sex and sleep and eat. We did walk into the little town or village, and that is where I first understood how much my wife hated mustard. From a street vendor, I bought two bratwurst. A very typical German midday snack. I put German mustard on each one, and we ended up getting into our first fight. She told me she didn't like mustard, and I kept trying to explain to her that the only way to eat German bratwurst was with mustard. She continued to explain that her cousin, when she was a little girl, had squirted mustard in her face while holding her down on the ground. Once again, I felt so sorry about her childhood. That endeared me to her even more.

The next day we took a short two-hour ride to Heidelberg, Germany, and stayed at the Hotel am Schloss. Our room had a skylight so that from the bed, you could see the castle ruins of Heidelberg. By the way, *schloss* means "castle" in German. It was magnificent making love in that hotel room with my wife on top of me and looking up at the castle ruins both day and night. After walking through the market the next morning in Heidelberg, we rode over to Strasbourg, France. We stayed at a nice little French hotel, and I was thankful that, with my small amount of French, my German came in quite handy, because the language there was mainly German with a little bit of French thrown in just to confuse you. After walking around the city, we had dinner at a little restaurant near the hotel. The waiter was not in any way covering up the fact that he was hitting on my wife. It was very uncomfortable, and the food he served me, which included a fresh prawn, tasted like someone had poured kerosene over my plate.

Very early in the morning, we headed over to Munich, Germany, and had a beautiful day sightseeing. We parked in the middle of the town square and walked to every tourist attraction that I had on my map. My favorite was a small park that held the tomb of the Unknown Soldier for Germany from World War II. I don't care who you are, every person has a deep and sincere loyalty to his or her own country. Right or wrong, a vast majority of Germans never knew anything about the atrocities that Hitler was committing. After World War I, they were searching for a leader who would take them out of destitution. Unfortunately, it was Hitler, who promised them a better life by reclaiming the land that Germany had lost after World War I. What a horrible and shameful mistake!

Late that afternoon, we left Munich, and as I had no hotel reservations we looked for a *Zimmer Frei*. We found a little country farmhouse, and the widow was such a sweet old woman. She spoke no English, and my German, at that time, was only about 75 percent good. She kept asking for pictures of our wedding; because of the short time, we had none, but she was so extremely happy that we would spend part of our honeymoon or *flitterwochen* at her home. In German, *flitter* means "high" or "fly" and *wochen* means "week." So basically, "your highest week." And that also meant your honeymoon.

We left the old farmhouse and took an uneventful ride down to Zurich, Switzerland. We stayed in the middle of the college district and spent the entire evening and the next day window-shopping. The following morning we took the most beautiful ride that I think a person can take on a motorcycle, and that is from Zurich to Innsbruck, Austria. Although you are in the mountains, the roads have been carved out so that you're really only traveling switchbacks through the foothills. You ride through deep green forest and heavy vegetation to roadways that have snow on each side. The sky is crystal blue, the grass and trees are deep green, and the snow is virgin white. Quite an unparalleled sight!

In Innsbruck, we stayed at the little hotel on the outskirts of town that had a Chinese restaurant on the first level. The Chinese food was actually pretty good! There was also a beautiful castle in Innsbruck that took us about forty-five minutes to walk up to. Along the way, we passed a small apartment complex, and I noticed that many of the women were sunbathing naked. My natural male eye couldn't help but look. Unfortunately, I got caught, and that was the second fight we ever had. After touring the castle, we decided to take the Harley into the city center and do some touring and window-shopping. In Europe, every city center is where the main church is located. All European cities have one at their city center, the largest and most well-attended church. It is usually surrounded by an incredibly large city square or a large paved opening where people could gather and pray, or listen to the local governmental procrastinators tell them what was going to happen in the near future. While Theresa and I were there and walking around the open square, we saw a man dressed in a suit and tie standing by himself but laughing hysterically. I had to see more. Theresa kept begging me not to go over there, but I was compelled. We watched this man for half an hour. He would stand there stone-faced and then instantly burst out laughing until he was doubled over with laughter. He would immediately stop laughing, stand up straight, and look perfectly normal. And then one minute later, he would burst out hysterically until he was doubled over and compact, and then within one minute he would instantly stop. I called him the Laughing Man. It was the only way I could describe him to my sister Gini, who was really the only one who would understand that I could find humor in a man who probably had Tourette's syndrome. May God have mercy on my soul.

As we left Innsbruck, heading back into Germany, we had another spectacular ride up through the Black Forest or *der Schwarzwald*. We found a small *Zimmer Frei* near the Neuschwanstein Castle. This castle is probably one of the most pristine and well-kept castles of its time in Germany. It was a wonderful tour and quite unforgettable with its beautiful views of the Black Forest. One of the things I remember is that the daughter of the owner of the room we were renting for the night looked exactly like an ex-girlfriend. She was tall and thin and had the tiniest buttocks you can imagine, yet extremely firm. I never said a thing, my wife never knew anything, but I was so horny that we made love like five times that night!

We ambled on the motorcycle all the way up to

Frankfurt that next day and dropped the Harley off at GmbH on Monday morning. We took a taxi and spent the night in a hotel near the Frankfurt International Airport. It was dramatically austere compared to the hotels and the homes we had stayed in during our trip. But we did get a good night's sleep after making love all night and had an uneventful flight home. It was the end of our honeymoon and the beginning of our marriage—something that I vowed I was deeply committed to working on for the rest of my life.

CHAPTER 14

TIMES THEY ARE A-CHANGING

CHUCK WAS GONE, AND I had taken over the direction of the most successful retail program that Harley-Davidson or any other corporation had ever accomplished. I was the king (at least in my own little world). I was interviewed by a dozen magazines and won the very prestigious Best in the Industry award from POPAI for outstanding merchandising achievement. Clark and I and my staff had a successful and thorough understanding of the dealer network in relation to what their retail needs were and how to help them accomplish everything they had ever dreamed of.

Enter Anne Tynan. She was hired by one of the upper executives, who met her as a result of who knows what. Maybe he met her on a plane. She was a skinny little woman. I knew her as a young child when I lived in Shorewood and she would visit a friend of mine down the street. Even as a seven-year-old, I knew there was something different about this woman. My childhood intuition turned out to be spot-on. She was named vice president of the brand.

Now what the hell is that? Immediately she was in charge of the marketing department, the PR department, the trademark department, and the store design department, which included me and my employees. She was unusual, in my mind. And if I had to tell you every story about the odd things that she tried to make us do, I would have to write another book. She seemed to me to be a chameleon. I always thought that she could make her way through the organization and come out on top.

I had to deal with her while also trying to concentrate on our Japanese subsidiary. I took several instructional courses on dealing with the protocols of working with the Japanese businessman and felt that I was well-versed and subsequently prepared for my first presentation to Harley-Davidson of Japan. My first meeting was quite intense, and even though I spent a day and a half after I arrived in Japan relaxing and meditating, I was still a little bit nervous. I woke up early that morning at sunrise. As I was drinking my hotel coffee, I looked out my window upon a Japanese garden that was sculpted perfectly. I was on the second floor, so I had a perfect view and was quite close. There was a man about eighty years old practicing tai chi. His slow and even, calculated moves were amazing. I thought about seeing the sunset in Lappeenranta, Finland, at two in the morning. And now I was in Tokyo watching a man practicing tai chi at sunrise. I really have had a wonderful life. And I was fully prepared to face the Japanese.

Little did I know how accurate the courses I took to prepare for a Japanese presentation had been. I was the only American to put on a presentation in a room filled with twenty Japanese businessmen around a huge conference table. As I knew they would, they shot down every idea I presented to them, but I was steadfast and assured them that there was no way they could do anything but accept our program as it was and deal with it the best way they could through their organization. After hours of nonstop badgering, they acquiesced and signed up for the program. I had now conquered Japan. Dealing with Japan and traveling throughout the country was not only wonderful but also educational.

My friendship with Clark Richey grew greater as time went on. I felt that Anne hated him, probably because he was not from New York City. She wanted me to find a way out of the contract with his company. I already had another company under contract so as to give the dealers a choice and create a bit of competition, which was the American way. Also, Clark's company could not handle the volume of remodeling projects in a timely manner. The district managers and I were continuing to sign up dealers at a record pace. At this point in time, I had well over half the dealers in the United States and 20 percent of the dealers internationally participating in the program. I went on vacation to Hawaii with my wife, Theresa, and one of my new employees, Chaz, and his wife. We stayed at my timeshare on the island of Kauai. We were having a wonderful time until I got an urgent message from my right-hand person in the department, Shelley, informing me that Clark had died unexpectedly. I was devastated. It took every fiber of my soul to write this letter to Clark's parents, dated May 3, 1994:

Dear Mr. and Mrs. Richey,
I am truly sorry for the loss of Clark. He was a person any parent would be extremely proud to

have as a son. Though I cannot make it to the funeral service, I wanted to send you this message. Feel free to share it with others or keep it only among your family members.

Clark Richey was one of the most wonderful men I ever knew. He was a dear friend of mine. Although business brought us together, he would have always remained my dear friend nonetheless. Clark and I enjoyed a friendship of mutual respect, hard work, business growth, and probably most important of all, lots of laughter. Clark had the rare ability to find humor in even the most difficult situations. His love of life was always apparent. His joy of living was easy to see for anyone who spent time with him. Clark always faced his weaknesses as well as his adversities the same way: head on ... faced the storm. I respected him for all of these attributes. I celebrate his life by the memories of our great friendship. I mourn the loss, but Clark always lived his life as he wanted. He saw more and did more than 99 percent of the rest of the population. Needless to say, Clark Richey will live as a legend to the Harley-Davidson dealer network for his creative design work contribution. He will live as a legend to me as a friend, a leader, a partner, and a real giant among others. He will be missed.

Once again, my deepest sympathy to you and the rest of the family.
Sincerely, Bob Michel

The letter from my boss to the dealer network dated May 2 was very typical of the type of things that she would say and do. I always thought that she disliked Clark very much. But her opening sentence was, "It is with great sadness that I inform you about the death of a very close friend to many of us in the Harley-Davidson family." As low as my thoughts were about her, they sank further. I and many of my coworkers were beginning to think differently about her.

Any employee who had worked in my division for a while was starting to realize that his or her job was on the line. It was becoming more and more obvious that one of the upper executives was the heir apparent to Rich Teerlink's job. Many people in the departments that reported to Anne were scrambling to find new positions, as was I. At that same time, an opening became available in a weeklong training program at the Massachusetts Institute of Technology. My wife, Theresa, happened to be in charge of coordinating the people who signed up and arranging their trips to Massachusetts. She helped me and got me signed up to attend the meeting along with a couple of other Harley-Davidson executives. I couldn't believe that I was going to attend MIT. I earned a certificate in Organizational Learning. That was in October of 1995. I also received a certificate for my Halloween Bash costume. It was for the ugliest costume. On one of our final days, O. J. Simpson was found not guilty of murder. I found it odd, but I understood the liberal position of MIT because they had televisions set up everywhere to view the verdict. Out of all my training and education during my time at Harley-Davidson, I have never learned more about organizations and how to treat people who work with you than I did during this weeklong process. I came away realizing that the only way to truly run an organization was in an inverted "V": all the employees were on top, and I was at the bottom. I would demand goals to meet the organization's expectations, but I was responsible for acquiring all and any resources necessary for my employees to accomplish their goals. I knew that Rich Teerlink understood this. But one of the upper executives who was in my class never had any concept of this. He was the king, and everything would be done according to his will. On one of our last nights, after the Halloween party, MIT took us on a bus trip out on the town to do a little barhopping. On the way home, one of the last things I remember, besides making out with some girl from the Merck Corporation, was dropping my pants and mooning motorists along the freeway. In my defense, I was dared by the staff of MIT to do this. When I woke up the next morning, I was certain that this would be another black nail in my coffin. I was sure I would be fired when word got back to Milwaukee.

CHAPTER 15

A BIG TRANSITION

THERE WAS A FAIRLY new guy who became the director of dealer development after spending some time in the sales department. His name was Bill, and he was a good man. He also happened to be one of the most honest and straight-shooting employees in the Motor Company. He originally came to Harley-Davidson from Ford Motor Company. His honesty also led to his only fault, and that was that he saw all the policies of the company in either black or white. I really did have a lot of respect for him. At that time, I remembered back to 1984 when the marketing department told me that they would only use black models in the catalog for the products that they were obsoleting. It was the 1984 Harley-Davidson version of diversification.

I could see the writing on the wall working with Anne and decided it was time for me to find a new job in the company. My department had already accomplished remodeling projects in over 750 dealerships out of 1,000 worldwide. I didn't see a lot of potential left in my position, and I felt that Anne was unbearable to work for given my personality. I worked with Bill and created a position in his department where I would be responsible for establishing parameters and policies for each dealership's physical location building size. I knew this wouldn't be an easy job, because it was starting from scratch and we had dealers who were in rural areas where the cost of construction was $100 per square foot and we had dealers in places like downtown San Francisco where construction was probably $1,000 per square foot and the property was in the millions of dollars.

I had secured my new position in the dealer development department, which was under the sales umbrella. In one of the multiple meetings where I was turning the department over to Anne, Shelley was with me and boldly took the opportunity to tell Anne that she was fully prepared to take over direction of the department. Without a millisecond of hesitation, Anne told her that she shouldn't have even bothered to apply because she would never meet Anne's requirements. Shelley's eye began to twitch, and I could see her career flashing before her eyes. Within the next couple of months after I left the position of manager for worldwide retail services, Shelley was also gone. She had gotten married to some guy and moved to Philadelphia. I felt bad for leaving my department under Anne's direction, but I had to move on and felt there was no other choice. Many of the other people in that division were feeling the same way, and apparently several of them actually had an influence on one of the upper executives. He began an inquiry into the specific activities that Anne was up to. Through a bunch of convoluted methods that seemed to be a way to protect Anne, Jeff Bleustein spent a couple of months interviewing all current employees in her division as well as me, because I had recently departed. I have no idea why Jeff included me, because I always felt that he did not like me and would never value my opinion as he had never valued my opinion in the past. To make a long story short, Anne left the company. She went on to divorce her husband, who was a pretty cool guy, and leave her two children with him. She then married a multimillionaire who was in charge of a financial division within Harley-Davidson. They would later buy a dealership in the south.

During the next several months, not only was I working on policies and procedures for the dealer network facilities, but I was also trying to find a Harley dealership that I could buy. I looked at the dealership in San Diego. I looked at the dealership in Madison, Wisconsin. I looked at the dealership in Annapolis, Maryland. I was also talking to another dealer who had recently gone through a divorce, and his wife had been his business partner in the dealership. The dealership was Milwaukee Harley-Davidson. It was located in a blighted area of town and the price was right. The only catch was that I could only buy 25 percent with an option to purchase the remaining stock in 2003. The negotiation lasted several months. Only my wife, Theresa, and some of my closest friends and district managers knew what I was trying to accomplish.

I started cashing in all my stock options and took out a second mortgage on my home, as well as borrowing some money from my mom. Theresa and I were little concerned with how the organization would respond to me being a dealer and her being an executive assistant to one of the VPs. I gave my thirty-day notice on April Fool's Day, 1996. I hand-delivered every copy of my notice to every executive in the organization. The only executive who did not congratulate me and show sincere happiness for my future success was Jeff Bluestein He wouldn't speak to me for the next two years. I personally believe it was because he could no longer have me under his thumb like a controlling despot. It wasn't until he became head honcho that he would even look at me or talk to me. I felt, *Isn't that a childish and foolish way to treat a dedicated employee who has been with your organization for nearly fifteen years?* That was that.

CHAPTER 16

FROM THE FRYING PAN INTO THE FIRE

IT'S HARD TO EXPLAIN how excited I was, dreaming about the prospect of my new adventure as a business owner in a Harley-Davidson dealership. Unfortunately, the confused management of Harley-Davidson didn't know how to deal with this situation. Within two days of submitting my 30 days notice, I was suspended because of a conflict of interest. This idea was initiated by some upper-management dickhead who felt it would be best if I was terminated immediately. I really didn't care because I was getting paid anyway, but it was a little bit embarrassing. Maybe more for the corporation because of the way they were treating a longtime and dedicated employee. I spent the time creating a strategic plan for the next several years of the dealership's business.

The Knuth brothers actually started the original Milwaukee Harley-Davidson dealership. They had two locations, one on the south side and one on the north side. My father recalled stories of being a young boy in the 1930s and standing at the window with his hands around his face so that he could see clearly and gaze at the beautiful machines that were on display in the showroom. He dreamed about owning a motorcycle like every young man does. The Knuth brothers got rid of the south-side dealership and later sold the north-side dealership, which was located on Fond du Lac Avenue, to a man who was married to one of the Davidsons. His last name was Afline. He subsequently sold the dealership to Paul Kegel and his wife.

Within the first week of working at the dealership and trying to get an understanding of what I needed to do, along with my responsibility of overseeing the building of a new facility, I started to see that there were serious problems with Paul. At the same time, I was negotiating a deal with the major music event and festival that is held in Milwaukee every year by the name of Summerfest. I didn't have a lot of negotiation power because the deal had been 90 percent completed by Paul and his girlfriend. We were only going to sell T-shirts and trinkets, and the rent they had agreed upon was way too high. By simple mathematics, there was no way we were going to make a single dollar of profit, because you can only sell so many T-shirts per minute. I thought that Paul and his girlfriend were starting to act more and more like crazy people. She came charging in one day accusing Paul of being addicted to cocaine and demanding that I take over all of the business checking accounts and turn all of Paul's personal banking accounts over to her. It was obvious, I thought, that she was also on cocaine. I don't have much experience with cocaine and only tried it a few times. I never liked it. Don't get me wrong, I love the high, but I felt that the low was not worth the high. I would rather drink booze.

As she was ranting and raving and making a scene in the showroom with her broken arm (in a cast from beating down the door at their home where Paul was hiding in fear), I decided I needed to make the only logical decision and physically remove her from the premises. Before I did that, I restrained her and told Paul to get his car and drive to his attorney's office and discuss the charges of domestic abuse she had made. After they were both gone and I got the staff to settle down, I put my head in my hands and wondered what the hell I had gotten myself into. My father had warned me to stay with the corporation and not go into business with a partner. My current district manager had warned me that Paul was an unusual guy. I second-guessed myself over and over again for the next many years. Paul was different, but we became friends.

Paul was arrested for what his girlfriend claimed to be domestic violence. I thought I knew the real story. She had a complete understanding of how to tell a story to the police so that they would believe that she had been abused, when I felt that it was Paul being abused. I saw the bruises and scratches, and I never saw a single mark on her. Paul told me that she would go as far as checking herself into a woman's shelter in the middle of the night swearing that she was being beaten on a daily basis. But once again, I never saw mark on her. Before we even moved into the new building, Paul fled and moved to Florida. Unfortunately, within weeks his girlfriend tracked him down. He told me that she was stalking him. I think she had a suspicion, as did I, that he was dating our office manager. As it turned out, that was true.

I was starting to feel like a gun to the head would be better than dealing with all of this bullshit. It was bringing tension into my relationship with Theresa, and our marriage was beginning to suffer. I was irritable and not a joy, by any means, to be around. She started going out without me and making excuses for working late. I was already working six or seven days a week from nine o'clock in the morning until about nine o'clock at night. I saw the writing on the wall. One night, before we even moved into the new building, Theresa didn't come home from a business meeting until about midnight. It had only been six months since I bought into the dealership. Anyway, I went to sleep that night and woke up in the morning alone. I got up and she was sleeping on the couch downstairs. I woke her up and asked her what was going on. And all she said was that she wanted a divorce. She didn't want to discuss anything. She got ready and left for work. I found all of her clothes from the night before hidden and covered with dog hair. It looked like my life had taken a major turn for the worse. I was confident in my career and my capabilities, but I wasn't sure I could handle my personal life at the same time. At that specific point in time, I really felt that I had no security with anything but my family and friends.

CHAPTER 17

TIMES GET WORSE AND TIMES GET BETTER

By the time Milwaukee Harley-Davidson relocated into our new building, Paul was in so much legal trouble with his girlfriend that he stayed out of state. He remained "Fabian," which means using strategies of delay in avoidance. Unfortunately, I believed that he couldn't see any picture of peace at all and decided that the way to handle the problem was to marry her. They bought a house in Florida, and at least I only had to deal with him from afar. It never got any better.

The staff and I moved into the new building and reopened after a two-day shutdown. There were staff members I knew I could rely on, and there were staff members I knew I could not rely on. I had a discussion with Paul at one point about the fact that a majority of the people who worked for us, though enthusiastic, would not be able to make the move from a small dealership to a large dealership at the level of professionalism I would require from them. Probably the hardest workers were Sandi and Lori. Lori worked part-time and then came on full time after the relocation. She also encouraged me to hire her daughter Kelly. Along with many others, she turned out to be one of the greatest assets at Milwaukee Harley-Davidson.

The office manager filed a lawsuit against Paul Kegel and Milwaukee Harley-Davidson for sexual harassment. We settled and paid about $75,000 for that. What a shame, because their relationship was mutual and it seemed obvious to me, in my small thought process, that she only did it for the money. Some of the other employees Paul had hired without any type of hiring process I had to discharge within the next year. Even though times were going extremely well and our sales had gone from one hundred motorcycles sold per year to three hundred, I had to continue to improve the quality of the staff and the dealership. Even though I had to dismiss everyone Paul had hired (except for a few), I made it clear to those remaining what my expectations were and that I had no tolerance for failure. I had already instituted an employee manual and an annual review procedure. I stayed with that religiously, and all the employees were well aware of what was expected from them. I established weekly staff meetings for all the managers and posted our weekly profit and loss statistics on the lunchroom bulletin board along with the meeting notes from the staff meeting for all employees to read.

That first year, Milwaukee Harley-Davidson was awarded Dealership of the Year by the prestigious industry magazine *Dealer News*. The dealership was on the front cover of the magazine, with me and Paul, who flew up from Florida for the photo shoot. I was feeling trapped, but I was glad to accept the award. Milwaukee Harley-Davidson had an honor that could never be taken away from us. I had weeded out the staff that would not make it during the transition and replaced them with what I certainly regarded as the best dealership staff in the world. But now remember, this was during the great times. When times changed, I knew that I would have to replace these people with real salespeople. The current staff was capable of being fantastically friendly and amiable with all of our customers. But as I talked about earlier, customers are fickle and are really only interested in the best price. Loyalty goes out the door if your price isn't bottom-floor.

My divorce was going horribly. Instead of settling for an amount that I thought was fair, Theresa was demanding half of my 401(k), my pension from Harley, and half of my value in Milwaukee Harley-Davidson. We had only been married for four years, and I believed, as did my family and friends, that she was only after the money. Who really knows? I ended up hiring several lawyers and, after two years, settled on the exact amount of money that I originally offered her. She was out a lot of money for her attorney's fees, but she still got away with a sweet deal for only four years. That's about $20,000 per year. There is no doubt that I was bitter about what she did and how she did it. In my mind, there was no excuse for that. I don't care who we are or where you're from.

I started dating an old flame of mine by the name of Candy. She was an incredibly beautiful woman with a statuesque physique. The only physical flaw she had was a brown tooth in the middle of her lower teeth. She never seemed to care about it or want to do anything about it. What a shame; otherwise, such a pretty girl. I felt like Jerry Seinfeld—I just couldn't get past that, nor could I mention it. The sex we had was always incredible, even from the time that I dated her when she was eighteen and I was twenty-two. The last time we made love was on her pool table in her basement, and I swear that is where I got my hernia from. I had to have hernia surgery right before the Harley-Davidson ninety-fifth anniversary. I was assured by my doctor, yeah right, that I would be fine within six weeks. I didn't recover for six months.

During the ninety-fifth anniversary, Milwaukee Harley-Davidson took in more cash than you could possibly imagine. I remember leaving the HOG rally with a two-by-three-by-four-foot box filled with cash. I needed a bodyguard to take the money back to the dealership at the end of the day and put it in the safe. Naturally, Paul took a huge bonus, even though he did no planning or manual labor. The reports I got about Paul and his wife were that they spent most of the time on the backside of the dealership smoking. I'm sure it was their substitute for doing other things.

On the final day of my divorce, my devoted staff made a voodoo doll with a picture of Theresa's face above my desk held by a rope and a noose. They stuck at least a hundred pins in the doll and left me a box full of pins to continue the ritual. My divorce was finally settled and Theresa went on to live her life out west with her new husband. He was such an interesting-looking guy; he looked just like her boyfriend from high school. Good for her and good riddance.

Chapter 18

ROUGH WATER AHEAD

My stepmother of twenty-five years had cancer. It slowly progressed despite treatment and invaded her entire body. She passed away peacefully under my father's gentle care in the middle of winter. I hadn't been a dealer for long, and as you know, I had been going through a difficult time with my partner, Paul, and trying to finalize the divorce with Theresa. My heart was broken, for I had a deep unfailing kinship with my father and he was devastated. Whenever a man who is fortunate enough to have a great father sees him crying, it is the same as a knife in your stomach. It was a wonderful funeral, and I cried like a seven-year-old girl at the words and display of emotion of my father. The only person who attended the funeral from Harley-Davidson corporate was my ex-boss Bill. He also expressed genuine condolences. I will never forget that.

I began playing golf with my father at least once a week. And every year at about the anniversary of my stepmother's death, I took him on a weeklong golfing trip with a couple of my brothers, Jim and David, to somewhere warm. I figured it was the least I could do to get his mind off of the passing of my stepmother. And isn't that what a good son and best friend should do?

I started dating after my divorce was finalized. I was very bitter and very cautious, with a lot of anger inside me. I stopped drinking for a while hoping that would curb the anxiety, but it didn't. I went to therapy and that didn't help either. I started dating this new woman. She was a very successful businesswoman and was tall, thin, and looked a little bit like Sandra Bullock. We dated for a while, but she was stopped twicc in one night for DUI, and we broke up shortly after that. She was also one of those women who, if the lighting was bad, turned from pretty to ugly. Hard to explain that, but it was like a *Seinfeld* episode.

Then I found a woman while searching on match. com who was a very elegant true blonde with brown eyes. We actually fell in love with each other. She was divorced and had a ten-year-old son. I only spent time with her on the weekends when her son was with his father. That relationship lasted a little over a year and ended for two reasons. One was that in the middle of the night while we were sleeping together, she had explosive diarrhea all over the bed as well as me. As she ran to the bathroom I kind of thought she would escape out the window and shimmy down the drain pipe to escape. I dealt with it as delicately as you would with a sick child. I kept assuring her that it was nothing more than an accident and the washing machine would take care of everything. I put clean sheets on the bed and tried to forget it ever happened. No way. Immediately after a vacation when I took her to the East Coast, she demanded that we get married or the relationship was over. I was stunned but not ready to commit to marriage after a year or so of dating, which actually was only spending every other weekend together.

I met another girl on match.com. We did a lot of things together and a lot of traveling. We went to Europe, Florida several times to visit her parents, San Diego, and even Hawaii to visit my buddy Jim and his wife. Unfortunately, I found out that for many years she had a website where she would perform completely nude acts as she was dictated by her paying customers. That relationship also ended abruptly, even though we still remain friends to this day.

I continued to deal with Paul, the bitterness of a failed marriage, and a long string of failed relationships. My drinking intensified; my seven o'clock martini was starting to turn into a six o'clock martini and that turned into a five o'clock martini and so on. It wasn't until the Harley-Davidson new model announcement meeting in New Orleans that I decided I was going to change my personal life. It was the first night, when most of the dealers party their brains out. But because the dealers were spread out among many hotels, there really wasn't much action in any particular hotel. It was pretty early, and the staff of Milwaukee Harley-Davidson and I decided to change things up and get a good night's sleep. As we were walking through the lobby, I ran into my friend Hal and his sons, and we all decided to go across the street to a local bar and get some drinks. One of the last things I remember was drinking so many shots of whiskey that I was starting to get hot and nauseated. I woke up the next day in my room with my feet on the floor, lying back on the bed with my pants around my ankles. I had a big contusion on my forehead, apparently from attempting to take my pants off while leaning forward and smashing my head on the TV table. When I found Hal the next day, I asked him what happened. After he explained, I remembered everything. It was my first blackout. He told me that as I was leaving the bar, I took off my shirt, and as I got into the revolving door I passed out. Because I was halfway in and halfway out, he kept pushing on the revolving door, crushing my ribs and causing intense bruising around my rib cage. He finally got me up and out, and by slinging my arm around his shoulder he buddy-walked me toward the hotel. On the way to the hotel, the local New Orleans police stopped us and tried to arrest me. Hal simply said, "Hey, there are plenty of drunks over there. I got this one." He dragged me to the hotel and put me in the elevator, where there was a dealer from Germany who spoke very little English. Hal told him to push me out when the elevator door opened on the sixth floor. I don't know how I found my room, but apparently my guardian angel was on my shoulder … again.

CHAPTER 19

THE WORKING MAN

I DEDICATE THE THOUGHTS in this chapter to my brothers and sisters, my mom and dad, my friends, the DMs, my designer store team, the Harley dealers, HDMC support staff, and others like Kid, Bozo, and Maggie at my dealership.

Hopefully everyone will meet and have dedicated friends. During my life, and as an employee and dealer, I was graced by having many extremely dedicated employees and associates. This chapter is about the several hundred people who helped my Harley career and dealership operate with extreme efficiency. I will tell you, as best as I can recall, how many people made a difference in the success of my personal life, the Motor Company, and the dealership. Some wore dresses; some wore suits (cheap or expensive). Most wore jeans and Harley shirts. Many had dirty hands from hard work on "the line." Didn't matter to me. If they worked hard and were dedicated, they had my respect and admiration.

I was raised by my father, a successful businessman,

and my mom, a nurse who worked her way through college during the Great Depression. All my brothers and sisters became successful in their chosen field of endeavor. All of my friends are successful, and most of them are doctors or lawyers. When I attended MIT, one message was clearly emphasized over and over: "Your employees are your single most important asset." My mom and dad, brothers and sisters and friends had already taught me that, but it was confirmed for me at MIT.

I have worked with thousands of people. I have worked for some people and some people have worked for me. I have also worked as a consultant to many others in the Harley community. I have also worked for my father. My father taught me to be kind and firm. He taught me to be aggressive and understanding. In the field of sales, he taught me to ask five basic questions:

1. "What are your greatest needs?"
2. "What is the fulfillment of these needs meant to accomplish?"
3. "What are the problems in regards to ascertaining fulfillment of these needs?"
4. "What is the worth of supplying the needs and solving the problem?"
5. "If I can come up with the solution, will you buy it from me?"

These were five simple questions to create a successful relationship with anyone. Simple process, honest, straightforward, and respectful of the understanding of another human being, whether personal or business.

I have worked with people of every education level. Whether they had a GED, high-school education, college degree, master's degree, or doctorate, I found that their education didn't matter. The best ideas and business-process concepts came from each and every level of people, without discrimination. The definition of the working man in my mind is someone who is dedicated to his job and not himself. As a side note, I wish to say that the people without the highest education were the best people to work with. They had common sense, a sense of loyalty, and no narcissistic traits. They truly were the salt of the earth. God bless them.

Working with people you have a true affinity for is wonderful. Working for despots is a living hell. Even before Harley, working for my dad, I had the best employees. They were hardworking and cared about me when I was going through tough times. When I started working for Harley-Davidson, there was a sense of family. Most of my coworkers would look out for each other. All things change over time. I saw a pattern: as some of my coworkers were promoted, their personalities changed, not for the better but for the worse. The increased power and responsibility took away their sense of humanity. When I began hiring people in the designer store program, I searched for people with experience and empathy. I knew they would need this to deal with the tremendous difficulty that our dealers would face during massive remodeling. Pam was my first hire. She had extensive experience in retailing and was very sweet and kind. That made her a perfect match. My next hire was Shelley. She was experienced, worldly, and adaptive. The rest of my crew was hired by including

Pam and Shelley in the interviews, and I relied heavily on their opinions. That was how I built my team. As I could see their confidence and capability growing, I allowed them to hire personnel to work for them. After all, I had trained them and had to rely on their judgment. Every one of those employees was incredibly dedicated. They worked long hours and traveled extensively despite the burdens it put on their families. The only employee I did not hire, who was hired for me by Jeff Bleustein, I ended up terminating for fudging her expense report.

As I mentioned before, when I took over partial ownership and management of Milwaukee Harley-Davidson, I knew that there would be a lot of personnel issues I would have to deal with. This issue was exacerbated by the fact that we were moving into a 36,000-square-foot building, leaving a 2,500-square-foot building. Times were changing, and they were changing quickly. My goal was to train and educate all employees, well knowing that most would not be able to make the transition. My decision to let people go was not based on money but on customer satisfaction. We were growing exponentially, and I gave the existing employees all the training and opportunity to meet those challenges. Those who couldn't were coached, trained, and finally warned that they must produce. If, after all that, they were not producing, I terminated them. But only after that process.

After many years at Harley-Davidson corporate, I humbly learned how intelligent the dealers and their staff were about their responsibilities. I admit that I was one of those people in the corporation who thought that the dealers and their staff didn't know what they were doing.

But after becoming a dealer, I realized I was completely wrong, and I apologize for my underestimation of the Harley-Davidson dealer network. During my years as a Harley dealer, I had the privilege of working with some of the most intelligent people I have ever met. Not just fellow dealers, but their employees and mine. I was also privileged to meet the customers of Harley-Davidson's final product, these people who had finally fulfilled an expectation they had dreamed about their entire life. I wish that more corporate executives could feel how I felt, making someone's dreams come true.

I can't take any of the credit for the experience that our customers at Milwaukee Harley-Davidson had while going through our buying process. Well, maybe I can. It began with an excellent hiring practice and a gut feeling about the people I was hiring in some management positions. Maggie was an outstanding office manager. At the time, Bob was an excellent sales manager. Until his untimely death, Skip was an excellent service manager. Buffalo Bob, the parts manager, was probably the best parts manager I ever knew. I had dedicated customer volunteers like Kid, Bozo, and many others who would give their personal time just to help the dealership and further the Harley feeling of brotherhood. These people worked selflessly because they loved the product and the enjoyment that it brought to them. In my inverted work pyramid, I owed everything to them. Some of these people even expressed that they would give their freedom or life for me! By about 1998, I had developed an excellent team at Milwaukee Harley-Davidson. The staff were all trained, and we had all the logical business processes in place. I was working with the real working man.

In 1986, there had been a major change in the direction of Harley-Davidson. The board of directors and the upper management made the choice to sell Harley stock on the American Stock Exchange. In my opinion, they had just sold their soul to the devil. It is said that one cannot be true to two masters. As the corporation marched through the '90s, I saw this to be true. I think it was almost impossible to balance employee satisfaction, customer satisfaction, corporate profits, and satisfying stockholders at the same time. The new millennium brought about many changes in business. Some were good; I believe most were bad. Especially in America, large corporations were beginning to look more at profit and the bottom line than at the big picture.

The theology of the seven deadly sins is well known. Of the seven deadly sins, pride, greed, lust, gluttony and envy are the five that best describe many corporations today. We've seen it year after year and read the horror stories in the newspapers. Government officials, government agencies, corporations, and other companies are giving up their souls and betraying those around them as a result of one of these sins.

Conversely, the Bible talks about the three theological gifts of grace from God. They are grace, hope, and charity. In the context of this book, I suggest that Harley-Davidson set an example to practice grace, hope for their employees, and charity to every person that the company is in contact with. In my simple mind, that is what good leaders do. Many would argue that it is more complicated than that, but I disagree. When one executive at the top is making millions and millions of dollars while destroying the lives of his employees and his employees' families, the company should reexamine its values and consider its karma.

These lines from the movie *It's a Wonderful Life* come to mind:

"You sit around here and you spin your little webs, and you think the whole world revolves around you and your money! Well, it doesn't, Mr. Potter! In the … In the whole vast configuration of things, I'd say you were nothing but a scurvy little spider!

"Just remember this, Mr. Potter, that this rabble you're talking about. They do most of the working and paying and living and dying in this community. Well, is it too much to have them work and pay and live and die in a couple of decent rooms and a bath? Anyway, my father didn't think so. People were human beings to him, but to you, a warped, frustrated old man, they're cattle. Well, in my book, he died a much richer man than you'll ever be."

CHAPTER 20

THE BUYOUT

IT WAS APPROACHING 2003, and my buyout was set for July by contract. By the grace of God, Harley-Davidson chose to change the date of the hundredth anniversary to September. That meant that Paul would not profit from my (heroic) efforts during the ten-day event.

Even though I was excited about finalizing the buyout, I had to conduct day-to-day business. I had an incredible staff at the dealership who were either handpicked by me or survived my critical transition from being a small mom-and-pop shop to a multimillion dollar retail business. Maggie was my right-hand person and office manager. She was the best I ever met out of all the top executive assistants I had ever known. She also learned Harley's dysfunctional computer system, and the only thing she lacked was Human Resources skills. Sandi and Lori were the best at motor clothes and merchandising. They worked closely together as equals studying buying patterns and sales and ordering merchandise with a budget in the millions per year. Bob was a good old guy in charge of the sales department. He was large and jolly but as faithful as the geyser in Yellowstone Park. Skip was my service manager who I hired from an auto dealership. He was a little more giving than I was, but I think that helped our customer-satisfaction scores. I had several different parts managers, but Buffalo Bob was the best. He was old school with long hair and a scraggly beard. He knew every part number by heart, and I want you to understand that is hundreds of thousands of part numbers. He was great with customers but hated computers and corporations. We had plenty of arguments about it, but that was okay. He was good. This incredible staff, while believing in me and trying to ignore Paul, pulled off some incredible dealership events.

One of the most memorable events was when Lori came up with the idea to bring the traveling wall of the Vietnam Veterans Memorial to Milwaukee Harley-Davidson. I was sold and gave her a budget and told her that she had whatever resources she needed to accomplish this honorable display and event. She made all the arrangements, along with Maggie and help from the rest of the management staff. The main guest speaker we would have was Gary George Wetzel. He was a Congressional Medal of Honor recipient in 1968 during America's occupation of Vietnam, and he was also a customer of ours. I would like to quote his citation. This was written in 2012 by the Congressional Medal of Honor Society:

Sp4c. Wetzel, 173rd assault Helicopter Company, distinguished himself by conspicuous gallantry and intrepidity at the risk of his life, above and beyond the call of duty. Sp4c. Wetzel was serving as a door gunner aboard a helicopter which was part of an insertion force trapped in a landing zone by an intense and deadly hostile fire. Sp4c. Wetzel was going to the aid of his aircraft commander when he was blown into a rice paddy and critically wounded by two enemy rockets that exploded just inches from his location. Although bleeding profusely due to the loss of his left arm and severe wounds in his right arm, chest, and left leg, Sp4c. Wetzel staggered back to his original position in his gun well and took the enemy forces under fire. His machine gun was the only weapon placing effective fire on the enemy at that time. Through a resolve that overcame the shock and intolerable pain of his injuries, Sp4c. Wetzel remained at his position until he had eliminated the automatic weapons in placement that had been inflicting casualties on the American troops and preventing them from moving against this strong enemy force. Refusing to attend to his own extensive wounds, he attempted to return to the aid of his aircraft commander but passed out from loss of blood. Regaining consciousness, he persisted in his efforts to drag himself to aid of his fellow crewmen. After an agonizing effort, he came to the side of the crew chief who was attempting to drag the wounded aircraft commander to the safety of a nearby dike. Unswerving in his devotion to his fellow man, Sp4c. Wetzel assisted his crew chief even though he lost consciousness once again during this action. Sp4c. Wetzel displayed extraordinary heroism in his efforts to aid his fellow crewmen. His gallant actions were in keeping with the highest traditions of the US Army and reflect great credit upon himself and the Armed Forces of his country.

Prior to introducing Gary at the main event, I tried to give a speech but was, for the first time, choked up on the stage, as I tried to give honor to my father who fought in World War II in Okinawa and my brother Tommy, who served just prior to the Vietnam War in the air force. And I talked about my close cousins Johnny and Chuck and their involvement in Vietnam, where Johnny was gravely injured in a mortar attack. It was a wonderful event for Milwaukee, and we had many thousands of visitors. It wasn't necessarily profitable, but it was worth every bit of time and every bit of money that we put into it. I salute you, Lori.

I contacted a company in Milwaukee that had a reputation for coordinating business buyouts. The president was my contact. At first I thought he was a pretty cool guy. He was married with kids and spoke about being extremely Catholic. He was a good-looking guy and well-dressed. Kind of like the guys in *Mad Men*. He was helping negotiate with different financial institutions from liability to complete the buyout according to the contract that Paul and I made in 1996. During the same time, my incredible and capable staff and I were preparing for the hundredth anniversary. Along with all this stuff and the blah, blah, blah of the news media, I had no option but to be involved in it all, as Milwaukee's premier dealership. I was interviewed about eight times by the TV networks, local newspapers, and trade magazines. Paul and I ended up on the cover of the exclusive motorcycle industry magazine *Dealer News*. We were featured as the place to be during the hundredth anniversary. It reminded me of 1996, where my design of the dealership won Milwaukee Harley-Davidson Dealer of the Year in a worldwide contest. Unfortunately, I had to share the glory with Paul, who had a grin on the front cover photo like the grin that Jim Carrey had on the cover of *How the Grinch Stole Christmas* DVD.

I continued to negotiate with Paul without much success because sales were through the roof. The company I hired to help with the buyout was able to convince a local bank to finance the buyout, and by July 11, 2003, I owned the dealership outright. That same day, I flew to Las Vegas for the 2004 new dealer announcement meeting. It was so hot that when I rented my car and pulled up to the checkout booth, I saw a crow with its mouth wide open panting for moisture. It reminded me of the story my dad told me about traveling from the Great Lakes Naval Academy through Texas and on to San Diego, where he would board the ship that would take him to Okinawa. Again, it was so hot outside, and when they stopped at a train station outside of San Antonio, he saw a blackbird with its mouth wide open panting for moisture. I was on a high and hired a hooker for the next five days. I thought it was a pretty good deal, because she would show up at my room at about four o'clock in the afternoon and by six o'clock I was ready to go out with my buddies. It was one of the best dealer shows I ever had. And maybe, just maybe, it was because Paul was out of my life once and for all.

CHAPTER 21

THREE VERY DIFFERENT RIDES

DURING THESE YEARS, I took three very different and unique motorcycle rides. One was a ride in and through Germany with a girlfriend. The next one was a few years later, by myself, through Germany, France, and Austria. And the last one was a motorcycle trip sponsored by Harley-Davidson Motor Company called the Dealer Ride. After each new model announcement meeting for the dealers (during the summer), Harley helped arrange a motorcycle ride for any dealer who wanted to participate. That particular ride was after the dealer show in San Diego in 2005, and the final destination was Hump, Nevada.

Trip Number One

My girlfriend and I had decided to take a motorcycle trip through southern Europe and then fly up to Norway, which was the land of her heritage, and spend a week in Oslo. We flew from Milwaukee to Frankfurt, arrived early in the morning, and went directly to GmbH, where we had a Harley classic touring motorcycle waiting for us. I had to pay for this rental because the vice president of customer enjoyment would no longer extend any type of courtesy to anyone who was not a Harley-Davidson employee. So even with fourteen years of dedication to the motor company, more than half of that in Europe, he refused to help out a brother and a former comrade.

The bike was a full dresser but was in very rough condition. There was a steady rain falling that morning, and I packed the motorcycle while my girlfriend enjoyed a cup of coffee in the beautiful dealership. With all of the luggage and her weight, I am sure that we were at the maximum capacity for that particular model. The poor condition of the motorcycle coupled with the weight and the rain made for a very unnerving ride. I could tell the bike was not handling well within three minutes after we left GmbH on our way toward Heidelberg, Germany, which was our first destination. After a few wrong turns, I managed to navigate my way onto the correct autobahn. The ride only took a couple of hours, but I was terrified because of the poor handling of the motorcycle. I couldn't wait to get to our hotel, park the motorcycle, and wait out the rain. We had scheduled two days in Heidelberg—the first day to recover from jet lag and the second to conduct our tourist examination of this beautiful village.

After we checked in and unpacked the motorcycle, we made love and took a short nap. When we woke up, there seemed to be a break in the rain, so we took advantage and rode the motorcycle into the center of the city where there was the usual German festival taking place. We had a couple beers and of course some local food and wandered around the festival for a couple hours. We made our way back to the motorcycle and I realized, with some panic, that I had inadvertently set the alarm system and had no idea how to unlock the motorcycle. I tried a couple different things and then realized that the alarm system would lock me out after a third failure. I stepped back for five minutes, and then with the most concentration I could muster I succeeded in disarming the security system on the bike. We headed back to the hotel after a short tour around town and had a wonderful night's sleep. That is always a good end to the first day of traveling and the beginning of a motorcycle adventure.

When we woke up, it was raining hard. The weather report had nothing but rain in the forecast for the entire region for the next five days. Considering that our planned route would keep us under this rain, we decided to stay in Heidelberg until the weather broke. The weather never broke during the entire rest of the motorcycle-rental time frame. I made the decision to cancel the trip into France, Switzerland, and Austria, coming back through southern Germany. It was a real heartbreak, and I had never had to cut out a major part of any vacation I'd ever taken in my life. Instead, we made the best of five days in Heidelberg, which turned out to be wonderful.

Heidelberg is the old capital of the Palatinate. It dates back to about the twelfth century. You are in a spectacular village nestled on the Neckar River in the southern German uplands. If I wanted to be stuck somewhere for five days, this would be the place. With the age and history of this city there were hundreds of places to visit. There were dozens of wonderful restaurants and beer gardens, and one of the most famous castles ruins in all of Germany.

The castle ruins, high on the hill above the town, are one of the noblest examples of the German Renaissance architecture. It was built between the fifteenth and sixteenth century and, because of its size and beauty, is definitely my favorite tourist stop in Europe. The day before we were ready to depart Frankfurt, we packed up the bike and took a leisurely ride to spend the day in the small town of Michelstadt. This is the same small town I had been in before, and I firmly believe that if I traced my ancestry, it would lead back to this town. We spent the night at a nice Frankfurt hotel and departed early in the morning for Oslo, Norway. It was still raining!

We flew from Frankfurt to Amsterdam, Holland. The Schiphol airport is the best airport in the world. If you ever need a layover on a flight that takes you over Europe, I strongly suggest that you pick that airport. It makes you feel like you want to party the entire time you are staying there. It does not make you feel like your layover is really a layover but more like a mini vacation at a high-tech shopping mall. I've been there several times, and I discover more things to see and more places to go inside this airport every single time. After our wonderful layover, we departed and arrived in Oslo, where her ancestors came from several generations ago.

The weather was quite a bit cooler, probably fifty to sixty degrees. We had reserved a quaint hotel in the middle of downtown Oslo. I had been to Oslo before but never really spent that much time hitting the local tourist attractions. We spent the next three days exploring every street in every attraction and every shopping area that we could. We spent most of our time down at the harbor that pretty much looked like any other harbor in a smaller town around the world. We ate the local food, we drank the local drinks, and we tried to immerse ourselves in the Oslo culture for several days. We really had a great time, even though we were not on a motorcycle.

Trip Number Two

In North America, the largest motorcycle show has always been held during January. For many decades it was in Cincinnati and was referred to as the Cincinnati Motorcycle Show. It had recently moved to Indianapolis. Every OEM was at the show, and anyone who produced anything for any type of motorcycle or all-terrain vehicle was present there with all of their gadgets, clothing, and ideas. It was a show that took several days to cover from end to end, even walking at a fast pace. I think it was in 2003 that I drove from Milwaukee to Cincinnati through snowy winter weather to attend the show. I was delayed by the weather and arrived at the opening banquet about half an hour late. I filled out a few forms, received my name tag, and headed toward my assigned table. To my surprise, my ex-partner's brother who owns the dealership in Rockford, Illinois, was also sitting at my table.

Within minutes of sitting down and exchanging greetings with the other eight people at the table, I heard my name being announced from the stage. They called out, "Is Bob Michel here? Is Bob Michel here?"

I looked at my ex-partner's brother and ask him what the hell that was all about. He said I had just won a trip. I asked, "What trip?"

He said, "The trip to Italy."

I said, "What trip to Italy?"

At that time, the announcer was just about to pick another name, and I jumped from my seat waving my arms and yelling, "I am here! I am here! I am here!"

As I approached the stage, I saw that the announcer and his guest were holding a poster of the international motorcycle show being held in Milan, Italy. They had pulled my name from the many forms I had filled out at registration, and I had won an all-expense-paid trip to Milan for two people as a VIP of the prestigious *Dealer News* magazine. Many celebrity-type photographs were taken of my acceptance of the trip, and I walked off the stage in a daze, not even really understanding what had just happened. During the dinner and the following reception, it started to sink in how lucky I really was. Also during the evening, I started planning my entire trip. I knew that I would use the trip as a springboard into another Northern European motorcycle trip for myself. I had already purchased the dealership from Paul and was the sole owner, and I knew that after the hundredth anniversary I would need some time to unwind and to recharge my batteries. This was absolutely perfect. The timing couldn't have been better. I couldn't have had better luck. I felt that God had blessed me.

A month or two before departing on the trip, I was still single and had no one to go with, and I decided that it would be a wonderful opportunity for my secretary, Erica, to go along with me and experience the motorcycle show as well as the pressure that the news media can bring upon people in the spotlight. She was the cutest thing. She was nineteen years old and had appeared in our motorcycle, babes, and bikes calendar. She was a very good employee and my intentions were honorable, even though my fantasies were different. She got her passport and helped me make all the arrangements. She and I would travel together to Milan, and after the show I would escort her back to the airport and get her on a plane, with my excess clothing, back to Milwaukee. I would then fly to Frankfurt, pick up a motorcycle at GmbH, and travel around Europe for another ten days.

The trip to Milan was wonderful. It was fun to fly to Europe with someone who had never done that before. You kind of feel sorry for people who don't have a lot of experience flying because you see how uncomfortable they are and how exhausted traveling makes you, even though you can barely sleep. As usual, the flight arrived in Milan early in the morning and our room at the hotel would not be available until three or four o'clock in the afternoon. It was a beautiful autumn day, and I decided that we should walk to the local park and just rest on the park benches. We found some park benches next to each other and lay down, and both of us fell asleep for about five hours. I couldn't believe it. I'm surprised we weren't mugged. I'm surprised she wasn't kidnapped. Waking up from a deep sleep like that, I was surprised we were alive. During the entire trip, the Italian men were relentlessly pursuing Erica because she was so beautiful and an American. The Italian women were pursuing me as well, but they were much more cautious, thinking that I was with Erica. As soon as they found out that she worked with me, they were unrelentingly trying to get me into bed.

The show was excellent, and we were treated like VIP

motorcycle legends. I kept reminding myself that I had just won a trip, and that was all it was. But we were treated so well by *Dealer News* magazine that I still have to bow down and thank them for everything they did for us. They even took us to a private showing of an opera at the Opera House of Milan, which was phenomenal. One evening, one of the Italian models who I had been talking to during the day had made arrangements to come to my room that night for a midnight rendezvous. This woman was absolutely beautiful. Her body was statuesque. Her facial beauty was classically Italian. Her eyes were hypnotizing. We made love until five in the morning. The only odd situation that came up during our entire visit was at a press conference dinner with all of the reporters; our host, *Dealer News* magazine; and several Milan political and government employees. Erica and I had ordered our drinks. She ordered a simple rum and coke. When it came, she took a drink and had a funny look on her face. I asked her how her drink was. And she said in a very loud voice that was heard by everyone, "This tastes like ass!" An immediate silence came over the group. I was mortified. But within two seconds, the entire table of twenty people burst into laughter that lasted several minutes.

We said our good-byes at the airport, and Erica and I went our separate ways. She flew to Milwaukee and I to Frankfurt. The end of one trip, and the beginning of another adventure for me on a motorcycle in Europe. The motorcycle I chose this time, because I was by myself, was a V-Rod, the fastest and best-handling motorcycle Harley-Davidson has ever made. I knew I had to travel light, and that is why I gave Erica my excess baggage. Post-9/11, she had difficulty explaining men's clothing in her luggage, but because she was so cute and a firecracker she made her way through security and arrived safely in Milwaukee. I still cringe at the thought of how she tried to explain men's boxer shorts and a jockstrap in her luggage!

I picked up the V-Rod and had already planned to wear a backpack because I knew that the small saddlebags under the V-Rod would not hold enough for a one-week trip. The backpack proved to be a challenge, especially at slow speeds. It was heavy, approximately twenty-five pounds. It also played out its physics at high speeds, especially when I would change lanes abruptly on the autobahn at one hundred mph! It took about an hour or so to adjust to it, but by the time I got to Heidelberg, I had the hang of it. I checked into my favorite hotel, Neckar River Hotel, and took a short nap. I woke up about five o'clock and prepared myself for a jog along the beautiful river, enjoying the exercise and the exquisite views. I jogged for about an hour, and when I returned, sweaty and worn, there was a group of four women speaking English on the patio in front of the hotel. I stopped to catch my breath and asked the same question all Americans ask: "Are you American?" They said yes, and that led into a long conversation about where we were all from and what we all did. Being the Harley guy and the magic that comes with that brought me into the group, and I could immediately feel sexual feelings from one particular woman who was blonde and thin and very pretty. I still don't recall her name, but her nickname was Tigger. As I found out that night, it was because she had a tattoo of Tigger by her pussy! We ended up spending the night together first of all as a group and later just Tigger and I. I can say this, she was a small-framed woman with small breasts, but they were the most perfect breasts that I have ever seen in my entire life, to this day.

I really hadn't made any plans as usual and was simply prepared to make my way through southern Europe and Germany on the bike, doing whatever I wanted and going wherever I wanted. A little bit of pussy can change your plans! They were planning on attending Oktoberfest in Munich within the next several days. I decided to follow the trail and abort my plans to go to Switzerland and ride through the Alps. I was slightly disappointed in myself, because I wanted to see how it would be riding the V-Rod that twisty journey and hairpin turns of the mountains that I so love to do. Even though we were separate, we all headed toward Munich to stay at a hotel on the northeast side of the city. I wasn't used to that; I normally stayed in the city center where all the action was, and all I had to do was walk. The girls left early in the morning, and after a long jog, I departed by checkout time and took a long circuitous route down to Munich. It was a beautiful ride, and I couldn't believe how beautiful the Bavarian beginning of the Black Forest is to see on a motorcycle traveling at leisure.

I had never been to Oktoberfest, even though I had wanted to attend many times. My schedule just never allowed me to make that type of trip at that time of year. We all climbed into a taxi and arrived decked out at Oktoberfest early in the afternoon. We sat at the big tables under the big tents at the big-name beer distributors and drank the big glasses of German beer. The beer was brought to us by the big German waitresses holding four glasses of that big beer in their big hands. I met a little German girl by the name of Emma who stole my heart for the evening. My German was good enough to try to seduce her, and her will was stronger than my persuasion. That was okay, because I had Tigger as a backup. I got so drunk that I could barely walk, and Tigger helped me back to get a taxi. We went back to the hotel room and after resting for a while, we had sex for a while and then passed out. We woke up the next morning and had more sex. The next day, I followed the girls in their rental car to the Neuschwanstein Castle in southern Germany in the Garmisch-Partenkirchen area. It is one of the most pristine and well-kept castles in all of Germany. You have probably seen photographs of this castle, as it is the personification of castles in your imagination. We toured the castle, had lunch in a small little Bavarian town, and headed back toward Munich. After a late dinner and drinks, Tigger and I made love all night, and the next morning I followed her to my next stop, which would be Würzburg, Germany. We stopped there momentarily and I kissed her good-bye. I wish I had gotten more information from her. Shortly after I returned to America, my computer crashed and all the information about her e-mail address was lost. I knew she was from around the Brooklyn area in New York City and that she was a police officer.

Würzburg is an incredible city. It is entirely surrounded by a twenty-foot-high stone wall. The wall contains hollow areas where the guards could protect the city from invaders. I'm sure the Great Wall of China is a spectacular sight. I have been to China once and have no interest in going there again, even though I would like to see Great Wall. I think I'll be happy with the *National Geographic* photographs and TV series on the subject. I spent the next day jogging around the city and the wall and shopping and doing all the things tourists do. The following day, I dropped the motorcycle off at GmbH, spent the night with an old girlfriend in Frankfurt, and departed the next morning for Milwaukee. That V-Rod to this day is my favorite ride.

Trip Number Three

After the 2006 annual summer dealer show, Harley-Davidson corporate arranged a ride for dealers. Any dealer could participate or not; it was a voluntary option. Each dealer chose a motorcycle that he knew would be shipped to his dealership for the upcoming model year and requested that that motorcycle be sent to the designated dealership in the hometown of the dealer show. That motorcycle would be delivered during the dealer show and prepared by the dealer for his ride to a final destination and subsequently shipped back to his dealership to ultimately sell as a new motorcycle that was executive-ridden. Again, we were riding from San Diego to Hump, Nevada, where my good friends JC and Marci owned the dealership. JC had been with me on a couple of trips through Europe, and his wife, Marci, was on that trip through southern Europe and to Tangiers with my sister.

As you probably now have an understanding about how much drinking goes on at the dealer shows, you will be able to put this story into better perspective after I describe the checklist that one had to go through to achieve utter disaster. The final evening party, which used to be called the president's dinner, was held atop the oceanfront Hyatt on the beach in San Diego. The weather was hot. Harley-Davidson had reduced the budget, and so they were only serving cheap wine and beer. The beer was cheap also. So in order for most of us to get a good buzz on, we would head down via the elevator to the first-floor bar and order some drinks, usually doubles, and head back up to participate in the festivities. Harley always did put on a good show for the dealers. All of my friends and I drank until closing time, which was two a.m. Pacific time, and a few of us had to get up at six a.m. for the ride to Hump. My buddy Jim and I made assurances to each other that we would wake each other up and meet down at the motorcycle pool at ten to six with all of our gear and be ready to ride. We were there shoulder to shoulder ready to ride at six a.m. I felt like shit and I think Jim did too, except he only had a couple beers and I drank about a gallon of vodka.

We had a police escort out of San Diego leading us to the highway heading north. It was hot already at seven o'clock in the morning, and I was already feeling nauseated. When we reached the San Diego city limits, we stopped for a rest stop and Jim and I had coffee and water. Because Jim lived there and was acclimated to and knowledgeable about the weather, he made me promise and commit to stopping every hour on the hour to drink water and take respite from the heat. The forecast for where we were going was to be up to 110 degrees. We were on our way to Big Bear Lake. I told Jim that I didn't feel well and did not want to ride with the rest of the group.

I asked him if he would stay with me. He's my buddy, and I knew that he would never leave my side. The rest of the group rode on and Jim stayed with me, and we took our time heading up north. Via cell phone, we were informed that because of forest fires near Big Bear Lake, that stopover had been canceled. We were told to proceed all the way up to Mammoth Lakes near Yosemite National Park. Not only was that unexpected, but feeling the way I did, it brought on a foreboding of disaster, as we had to ride an extra five hours through the Mojave Desert. The temperature in the Mojave Desert would be 125 degrees.

Whenever something goes wrong, it is not one single incident, it is a combination of actions that result in disaster. So let's start the checklist:

1. Drink heavily all night long before a motorcycle ride.
2. Only get about four hours sleep.
3. Eat absolutely nothing the night of the party or the next morning.
4. Take your motorcycle out into the desert and ride for eight hours in temperatures that range from 90 to 125 degrees.

I'd checked every box on the list and was definitely headed for disaster. One of the last things I remember is stopping for lunch and having a small salad because I felt sick to my stomach, and I bought a postcard to send to my mother. I filled out the postcard and naturally told my mother that I loved and missed her and mailed it from that rest stop before Jim and I continued on our way.

We traveled through the Mojave Desert, and I was struggling and struggling. I felt myself drifting out of my ability to stay focused and alert and my ability to stay conscious. Our last stop, I must have drank at least one quart of water. We filled up our water bottles and headed out on the road as Jim and I had done a hundred times before, but never in such intense heat and ungodly, unbearable conditions. As I mentioned before, Jim and I had agreed that we would stop every hour on the hour, but the next stop was about an hour and a half. I made it about forty-five minutes, and I started to hallucinate and black out. With every fiber of my being and an intense determination, I endeavored to persevere and ride on. There came a point where I realized that I no longer could do what I was doing, and by the grace of God it came upon me that I had to stop within seconds. I had the consciousness to put on my right turn signal and downshift as fast as I could. I could barely put the kickstand down, and I fell off the motorcycle after turning it off. It took Jim about a minute to realize that something was wrong, and he made a U-turn and came back to help. By this time, I was already laying on the ground quietly suffering from the effects of heatstroke. I had completed my checklist. Jim had no water left, and I had no water except for one inch in a small bottle that he poured on my head, and it was like pouring boiling water on me. There was no shade in sight and certainly not a shrub to hide behind and hope for shade. I could not breathe, and my world grew smaller by the second. Jim was really freaking out, and I started to feel that everything would be okay because I could just die now. My vision became myopic, and I slowly slipped into unconsciousness waiting for either God or the Grim Reaper.

At approximately the same time that I lost consciousness, I heard Jim yelling, "Help, help, help us!" We had not passed a single vehicle on that highway for an hour, and all of a sudden there was a California Highway Patrol car pulled up behind us. Over her loudspeaker she asked, "Do you boys need help?"

Jim screamed, "Yes, my buddy needs help right now!"

They both dragged me into the back seat of the squad car. She had no water, and her air-conditioner in the heat of the Mojave Desert kept the car at about a hundred degrees. She tried the best she could to race up and down the highway to get the air-conditioning to increase. Every time she made a U-turn, I was prepared to die from nausea and dehydration.

I kept saying, "I need a hospital."

She kept saying, "There is no hospital within a hundred miles of here."

I knew that I was going to die. California Highway Patrol officer Jamie Olthoff saved my life that day! As fast as she could drive, safely, she took me to the next town, where she helped me get aid at a gas station where they gave me ice bags and Jim got me Gatorade. I stayed there inside the air-conditioned gas station for several hours. Jim and officer Olthoff shuttled back and forth to retrieve our motorcycles. After about five hours, and several hours after California Highway Patrol officer Jamie Olthoff departed, I had enough fortitude to try to get back on the motorcycle and ride with Jim to our destination near Yosemite National Park. Two months later, I sent California Highway Patrol officer Jamie Olthoff a full set of Harley-Davidson patio furniture that was manufactured by my good friends at Ace, Inc., with a card expressing my gratitude for her saving my life. To this day, she probably thinks it was in the line of duty, but from my perspective, she saved my life.

Before I got on the bike this time, I soaked my T-shirt in water and put my leather jacket on, and then Jim and I continued our ride. I felt very weak and drained. We made our way by the grace of God all the way up to the foothills of Yosemite National Park. The weather was cool and I felt 50 percent better. We got to the hotel and after a brief rest, we were at the bar drinking to life and how great it is and how fragile it is. It can only take one occurrence in your life where you check every item on the checklist of disaster to truly create a disaster.

The next day, after feeling like I had been born again, I took a ride with Jim through Yosemite Valley and up into the mountains. It was spectacular. Except for the fact that there are no guardrails along the highest parts of the mountain, I had a wonderful ride. The drop-offs, if you're on a motorcycle, are exacerbated by the fact that you have absolutely no protection. In a car, you at least have metal around you. On a motorcycle, there is nothing protecting you. As you get older, your phobias can grow stronger, and my fear of heights had done just that. The ride was energizing and rejuvenating as well as terrifying. Jim and I made our way to Hump, taking hundreds of pictures as most buddies do all the way along the journey. Again, it's the journey, not the destination. We arrived in Hump and the heat wasn't as bad as it was in the Mojave Desert, give or take a hundred degrees. But I was really looking forward to seeing my great friends JC and Marci. We had a good party that night. Jim left earlier that day, and so I was alone and decided to hook up with one of the single women who was on the ride with another dealer. The whole group had a few drinks, but they were tired and prepared to go home, so an early night of sex made for a good night of sleep. I don't even remember her name.

In the meantime, there were storms brewing in the Midwest that were horrific. All flights from the West Coast to the Midwest were canceled. So instead of flying out of Hump, I had to get a rental car with a couple of other dealers and drive to Sacramento, where I turned the car over to another dealer from Chicago who continued on with the car to San Francisco where he could get back to the Midwest. I love Sacramento, and so I spent the night there and went down to the riverfront and found a girl who happened to love Harleys and took her back to my hotel and did screw the breath out of her. Never had that happen before, but she thanked me over and over again. Don't know anything about her, don't know her name, all I know is what we did. Finally made it back home, and if you've ever had heat exhaustion, be very careful, because it will be with you for the rest of your life.

I dedicate this chapter to my guardian angel, California Highway Patrol officer Jamie Olthoff.

CHAPTER 22

IT WAS ALL A LIE

A MAJORITY OF HARLEY-DAVIDSON dealers were becoming more and more disgruntled with the company's upper management. Even the Securities and Exchange Commission (SEC) had investigated upper management for violating laws against insider trading. Nobody was found guilty, and of course that would be the case. Harley had a built-in way of knowing exactly what their sales and profits would be for every quarter. The dealer contract required that each dealer take whatever number of motorcycles the company mandated. By knowing their exact sales and having control over their expenses, it was easy to project exactly what profits would be for any particular month. So even though upper management did this, selling their stock options at a tremendous profit, there was nothing that could be done. Trust can be earned and trust can be destroyed, and the upper management of Harley-Davidson was destroying the trust of the entire dealer network worldwide.

Our fearless leader, one of the upper executives, stood

on the stage more than once and promised the dealers that Harley-Davidson Motor Company would not produce one more motorcycle than the dealer network could sell. That all sounded good, but I remembered back to the old days and knew that eventually, even if the dealers lost thousands of dollars per motorcycle, they could sell every motorcycle they had. That was a hollow promise. The company continued to increase manufacturing capabilities as well as building new facilities and warehouses to feed the greed that Jeff Bleustein felt was necessary to impress the corporate/private investor via the stock market. He had no empathy for the dealer network, and in fact despised them—me—as much as he'd always despised the district managers, because in his mind they'd accomplished more than he had. No one could ever figure it out, but when he left the company, I guarantee there was not a single person who was sorry he was gone. If anyone knows of someone who was, please send me his or her name.

I received a letter from a former employee and coworker at Harley-Davidson Motor Company, Shelley. It was a wonderful letter, and she apologized for how she had acted during the last year of our business relationship. I won't go into details, but it was a perfect enough letter that I forgave her, and we have remained very close friends ever since. She had moved back to Milwaukee and was in the process of a divorce. I hired her to manage all of the dealership affairs down at the Summerfest grounds, where there would be hundreds of thousands of customers. She performed at a high level, as she had in the past; she performed at 110 percent.

During the hundredth anniversary, we made more

money than you could imagine, but because of Harley-Davidson's restrictions—specifically the marketing department—we were greatly limited in what we could sell. That probably cut each dealer in the Milwaukee area's net profit by $100,000. In Harley's eyes, that doesn't mean anything, but for each one of us dealers, that can often mean a "make it or break it" year. Many people think that Harley-Davidson dealers are rich. Not so. We live on a margin that is smaller than any other retailer that I am aware of. Most clothing manufacturers have a 100 percent margin; Harley-Davidson dealers have a 25 percent margin. Same with margins on parts and accessories. Only on T-shirts, one of our biggest commodities, are we are lucky if we can get 100 percent. When you do the math and add to the fact that the company-mandated dealers had to increase their facility sizes to tens of thousands of feet, at tremendous cost to them, the numbers don't turn out very well. Dealers were starting to lose money, and immediately after the hundredth anniversary sales began to drop. For my dealership, gross sales dropped by 25 percent. There was no one at Harley-Davidson who had any advice about what to do and how to resolve the situation.

The hundredth anniversary was a bust in many ways—mainly from a marketing perspective. First of all, the marketing geniuses had an idea that if they could hold events all around the world in major cities and showcase big-name, current, and popular bands, they would attract new customers. Everyone except them knew that non-motorcyclists do not go to Harley-Davidson events. The events were a flop all around the world. The company wasted a lot of time and dollars in a futile attempt to attract new and younger customers. And of course, there was Elton John as the secret performer for the hundredth anniversary surprise. I know it wasn't the company's fault, as the original performer checked himself into rehab a couple of weeks before the major event. Harley had been promoting the best performer in the world to be at this event, and they ended up with Elton John. Out of a million choices, I don't think a single dealer or customer would have chosen him. It was a travesty.

I left for Europe on my trip to Milan shortly after the hundredth anniversary. I began thinking about the fact that the dealership had grown so large that I probably needed a general manager or a partner. I thought about my office manager, Maggie. Also, I considered a good friend of mine and ex-employee at the Motor Company, Chaz. He was now managing a dealership in Michigan. I decided to try to convince Chaz to become my partner and buy me out over ten years. Even though our sales immediately began to drop as a result of the overproduction that was mandated by one of the upper executives, I felt within a few years things would even out. Many other dealers felt the same way. But it never really happened until 2012. Many sole proprietors lost almost everything they had. But Harley corporate management made many millions before they left the company. Funny, first on the list of the companies' values is to tell the truth ...

Chaz and his wife and I negotiated for what seemed to be a small period of time. We agreed upon a settlement that was satisfactory to all of us. Unfortunately, we used the same broker who I had used before, Jim Swinefelt. I was starting to get a weird feeling about this guy. First of all, he was always talking about how he had screwed his ex-partner and how easy it was to do because he simply drove the business into the ground after he bought it and then offered the guy pennies on the dollar to buy him out, or everyone would lose everything.

There was something else about the guy. He was a clean-cut guy. He was a family man with three kids and a wife. He claimed to be a devout Catholic, but he never talked about God even when I did. And every time I went to his office, the first thing he wanted to show me, with great excitement, was the latest pornographic videos that he had viewed in recent days. As usual, I should've gotten a clue by what he was doing and the way he was acting instead of the way he was talking. This guy was a walking enigma.

Chaz and I consummated our deal for the buyout with the understanding that he would slowly take over all the responsibilities of the dealership and buy me out within the next five years. It started as a great idea, but Chaz was not the partner I thought he would be, especially in the area of Human Resources. He proved to be very incompetent in dealing with the employees.

CHAPTER 23

THE UNGRATEFUL GUTTERSNIPE

THIS WAS NEAR THE beginning of the end, and it also led to a new beginning in my life. The date was October 31, 2006—Halloween—and I was on a Mediterranean cruise sponsored by Harley-Davidson Motor Company. Milwaukee Harley-Davidson had won the dealer incentive trip for the year by exceeding our corporate/dealership goal expectations. The trip, for me, started a few days before when I took an early flight to Nice, France, to spend a little time by myself and for getting over the jet lag. If you know anything about overseas flights, they usually leave the United States in the afternoon and arrive in Europe in the early morning. It's always a difficult flight because you're tired, jet-lagged, and everything seems a little surreal. Anyway, I took a taxi to my hotel, which was in Monaco, and probably arrived at about one o'clock in the afternoon. The ride was beautiful, especially if you weren't driving but in the backseat of a taxi. I got to experience the roadway that the Le Mans race is run on. The hills and hairpin turns are really amazing. You have the Mediterranean on one side and the hills and bluffs on the other. There are mainly hotels and tourist areas along the way, including the marina—absolutely fantastic view of very large yachts. Very beautiful. I had been there before, as I mentioned in chapter 12. So I tried to check into my hotel room and showed them my passport and explained that I had a reservation for Robert Michel. Now in French, my last name would be spelled "Michelle." So the frogman says to me in his deep French-accented English, "We have no reservations for Michelle Rohbear."

I said, "No, it's Robert Michel."

He said, "No! We have no reservation for Michelle Rohbear."

Well, this went on, back and forth, for three or four minutes. I finally said, "I know who I am, damn it! My name is Robert Michel," and I had to dig through my luggage to get the reservation number.

He looked at it, he checked in the computer, and he said, "Oh! I see. You are Robert Michel." At this point, I was just so tired that I looked at him and nodded my head yes. "You cannot check in until four p.m.," he said. Frogs!

Well, my room wasn't ready, so I checked my bags at baggage claim in the hotel and decided to go for a walk along the sea. I'd left Wisconsin at the end of October, so I was dressed in a black long-sleeved turtleneck, and here I was in Monaco and it was about seventy-five to eighty degrees. I had no other clothes to change into. I was on the beach and walked for about three or four miles, sweating my ass off. Of course, there were some nice areas where there were topless sunbathers (always a nice added touch). At any rate, I walked around for three or four hours, went back to the hotel, checked into my room, and took a nap. Of course, I had to hang up all my clothes, make sure everything was neat and wrinkle-free. Then, lo and behold, after my nap, my good friends (and Harley dealers) from San Antonio, Texas, called and wanted to know if I would meet them for dinner. They happened to be right down in front of my hotel at a restaurant on the marina. They also had arrived early to spend a few days before going on the cruise. I went downstairs and met Hal and his wife, and their son and his wife, and we ate and drank and subsequently took a taxi up to a beautiful hillside overlooking the marina and continued to drink and snack on hors d'oeuvres until late that evening, when we went to the small center of town. We also went into the famous Monte Carlo Casino. So very beautiful at night, it is palace-like, accented with beautiful old architecture. Outside on the streets, the valet parking area was filled with Jaguars, Mercedes, Austin Martins, and Ferraris. We spent the rest of our night donating our hard-earned money to the French. Fucking French!

We spent the next several days just hanging out, walking around the area where the city had a little carnival, and just enjoying the weather and the time together, laughing and joking. I decided to go watch the changing of the guard at the Monaco palace. The tourist crowd wasn't very heavy, and I got to walk around the entire area of old town. I bumped into Hal and his wife and we had a couple more drinks, some wine, and a little light lunch outside a nice café that was actually quite nice and peaceful. The next morning, I packed my bags to taxi over to the cruise ship. Checked my bags in and waited for boarding time. I ran into many dealers who were friends of mine, as they were also walking toward embarkation on the cruise ship. It looked absolutely beautiful, and I was actually excited to go on the ship and have a nice relaxing week enjoying old friends and coworkers from Harley-Davidson Motor Company and hopefully be able to work out every day and maybe even do some sunbathing. Well, that turned out to be a joke, because the temperature never got above sixty-five degrees the entire cruise. Most of the dealers ended up in the bars, casinos, and onboard shops, and going on excursions at the ports of call where we stopped.

The trip did start out pretty uneventfully. We started heading down the Costa del Sol, which is the east side of Spain, and on October 30—no, it was October 31—our port of call was Barcelona. I went with friends toward the shopping-district street in Barcelona, down the boulevard, which is essentially a very large and long flea market. Probably the most amazing sight, which Americans find distasteful, is the butcher shops. There are all kinds of meats, and skinned animals hanging in the air … it is actually rather disgusting. There are tens of thousands of flies everywhere in these butcher shops, and naturally the one place they love to land is on the meat. There are whole chickens, fish, pigs, lamb, sausage of every type, and many other European "culinary delights" in these butcher shops. Well, after walking about fifty miles through Barcelona, it was time to head back to the ship. We all went back to our rooms after a drink at the bar and got cleaned up for an evening of celebration, Harley-Davidson style.

And then it happened. It was about eleven o'clock at

night, and I was sitting at the bar with my friend Rugby. I noticed there was a woman with her back to me. She was talking loudly, and she didn't notice us until Rugby tapped her on the shoulder, interrupted her, and said, "I would like to introduce you to my friend Bob." She turned around and looked at me and my heart stopped! Now I don't know if you believe in love at first sight, but at that exact instant, I think I fell absolutely in love. I have not had that feeling since the day that I met my ex-wife (bad omen). I was absolutely, totally, and completely in love. And then I saw a wedding ring. It felt like my heart dropped from my chest to my stomach. How, in one second, could I be heartbroken? Dana was sitting with her mother, as I found out, and Dana introduced me to her. I figured, well, that's okay, I wasn't looking for anyone anyway. We drank the night away just talking about little things. You know, the usual bar talk—what do you do for a living, where do you live, have any children, how long have you been with Harley-Davidson, do you like the new allocation program? Blah, blah, blah. Her mother decided that it was time to turn in, but Dana and I were actually having quite a great conversation, so she decided to stay. Well, one drink led to another and then to another and then to another, and pretty soon it was bar time. Time to take a walk around the ship.

And this is where it started to get interesting. We walked around talking, and I was trying to play it cool, but I could also sense that she was trying to play it cool. She wore a cheap, clinging dress. She was a bit short for me and had a little bit of a square body—I could tell she had a little bit of a gut, the flabby stomach. She also had a skinny hook nose. But to me, she was beautiful. Stunning. Gentle. Exciting. We walked into the library on the boat, and we were talking about the type of books she liked to read. I told her that I loved to read aloud and was very good at it. I picked out a book and asked her if she would like to hear me read. She said yes, and then she kissed me. She kissed me long and hard! I was shocked. I went to sit down in a chair in the library, and she responded by lifting up her skirt and bending over so that I could see what God gave her. She hesitated, and then she sat on my lap. She put her head in my neck and asked me to read to her. Before I read to her, I warned her to be careful. "There are cameras everywhere onboard," I said. I read to her for about five minutes, and then the talking started to get a little more serious. She asked me if I was married, and I said no. I asked her about her ring, and she said she was married but separated. I later found out this was not totally true. She had been separated but was back living with her husband and her four-year-old son. Apparently they had "kind of" reconciled. Well, she asked me to walk her back to her stateroom. Her room was not far away, but it took us about half an hour to get there, as we stopped many times to make out. We passionately kissed goodnight but promised to see each other the next day. I said goodnight and walked back to my room with the excited lighthearted feeling of a young man in love. That was the beginning.

The entire next day, I couldn't help but wonder how I had never seen this beautiful woman ever before. She claimed to have been at every dealer show, and even in Milwaukee on many occasions. She knew many of the same people that I knew, and even some of my closest friends. How? How, after many years, had we never bumped into each other? In my mind, I retraced every step I could remember at each dealer show, down every aisle in every bar at every lunch and every seminar, and I knew I had never seen her before. Apparently, we had each been looking one way while the other was looking the other way. While I was walking up one aisle at the dealer show, she must have been walking down the next aisle. Why did the fates decide now was the time to bring us together? I guess it didn't matter, because I was in love.

That night, she came back to my room for some champagne. We decided to watch a movie, and she was afraid to lay down on the bed with her nice dress. I told her if she wanted, she could put on my bathrobe and hang up her dress. I didn't think she would fall for that line, but before I could blink she was out of that dress and in the bathrobe. Well, before the movie was over, we were making out, which led to wild passionate love! We lost track of how many times we made love. She fell asleep in my arms, and I had never felt so wonderful in my entire life. I didn't want to sleep, I didn't even want to close my eyes, I just wanted to look at her beautiful face. She woke up very late, probably four in the morning, and after a goodnight kiss, she went back to her stateroom.

The next day, many people were taking an excursion into San Tropez. The harbor water was pretty choppy, and with the beautiful backdrop of this lovely little town, a dozen or so people could board the small tugboats that rumbled and belched out a horrible diesel odor. So even if you weren't hungover, it made you sick to your stomach.

I woke up late, got on the last tugboat, and hung around San Tropez for a couple hours. I bought a few souvenirs, had a few beers, and headed back to the cruise ship. There I found her at the bar with her mom and a dear friend of ours, Diane from North Dakota. We proceeded to get liquored up and decided to take our drinks and go watch the people doing aerobics. We sat down to watch with our drinks and began to laugh. We laughed and laughed and laughed and then got kicked out! You would have to know Diane. We all split up, as we all had our separate dinner reservations. Dana and I promised to meet later that evening after dinner. As it turned out, I was having dinner with my friends, and I looked up and there was my babe and her mother having dinner two tables from me. She did not want her mother to know about us. But she still couldn't help herself from looking up at me every minute or two. After dinner, I went to my room and dressed for the evening, putting on my blue jeans, a crisp blue-and-white striped shirt, and a navy sport coat. At the designated place and time to meet, I waited from eleven p.m. until about one thirty in the morning. This luxury cruise served late night dinners. I knew she would be there, but where was she? Another friend of ours from Tennessee—her name was Cherie—came out and asked me to join her group for dinner. I explained my situation, leaving out many details, until she realized who I was talking about. When she realized I was talking about this specific girl, she was almost as excited as I was. She thought this hook-up was perfect. Well, Cherie was right! Dana had said with confidence that she would be here … and she finally did show up. She said she had been so hungover that day, along with the tugboat ride, that it had made her sick and she fell asleep after dinner, by accident. We snuck back to my room and made love for hours in every position, doing everything possible, examining every inch of our bodies. When we were done, we would start all over again. She loved to be on top, and I loved it too. The rest of the trip was like that every single night. I have never made love as many times in so few days as I did with her on that trip.

God, I was in love! One of the nights we decided to go to my stateroom at about eleven p.m. On the way through the hallways, she kept grabbing me and kissing me, and then she said, "Let's go into the laundry room." Well, this laundry room was right next to her stateroom, where her mother was sleeping. We were making out like crazy, and she wanted me to take my pants off and make love to her right there. I said that she was crazy because somebody could walk in at any moment, and I knew that she did not want anyone to know about us. Then I said, "What if your mom comes in to do laundry?" She told me not to worry, that her mother would never be up this late doing laundry. And she unzipped my pants and started to talk at my manhood, telling him what she was going to do. I lifted up her sweater to fondle her beautiful breasts. At that exact moment the door opened and someone walked in. I was mortified … it was her mother! Of all the people, in all the places anywhere on this ship, how could it be her mother, in here? I didn't know what to do, but in a split second I simply said, "I have to go!" And I turned around and walked out. She came to my room later that night and said her mother never said a word to her about the incident. We made love like wild animals again and again and again and again!

She was unlike any woman I had ever met. I guess, to start, she had a young child. So her breasts were a bit saggy and her stomach had stretch marks. But I didn't care, I loved them. I loved everything about her. As the cruise was slowly coming to our debarkation in Rome, we made each other a promise that we would talk as soon as she got back to Texas. I had already planned to stay in Rome for about four days and fly my partner, Chaz, and his wife in for some sightseeing. My friend Hal and his family would also be there. It was with great angst and a heavy heart that my new gal and I said good-bye. I knew what I wanted, but I wasn't sure about her. I called her the very next day from my hotel room in Rome. I was staying right next to the Coliseum, and I had never been so excited to talk to anyone, ever. I called her once or twice a day for the next three days. I had a wonderful time in Rome. It should've been a week. It was one of the few great cities I had never seen but had always wanted to. Rome did not disappoint me. It was a fantastic city, and I would recommend it to anyone who had to pick one city in Europe to visit.

I flew back to the United States with great anticipation of new love. Planning and wondering: How can I make this work? Will it work? Did she want it to work? I would find out very soon, as we began talking five or six times a day. I would send her e-mails, she would send me cards, and she would send me pictures and love letters and cute little notes. I couldn't get her off of my mind. It was time to plan a visit to Texas. My current girlfriend had moved out upon my return. She left a note stating that I had chosen the bottle over her. Not actually, but I ignored her when I returned from my trip and stayed up late drinking and texting or talking to my new love interest. As the facts were that Dana was still married and living at home with her husband and her son, Texas might be risky. So we decided it would be best for her to visit me in Milwaukee. In thirty short days, she had separated from her husband, moved out with her son, and had an apartment of her own. She decided that she would spend her birthday, in December, in the frozen tundra of Wisconsin. Under a shroud of secrecy she planned the trip, I paid for it, and she flew to Chicago, where I picked her up in a stretch limousine. I had champagne, fruit, and cheese and crackers. We drank and made out the whole way to Milwaukee, to my home in the beautiful northern suburbs. She was impressed by my home, a huge five-bedroom, three-and-a-half bath, six thousand square feet ... Boy, that's funny, I just realized I was using a term that everyone in Texas seemed to be impressed with—square footage! Most people don't talk about the square footage of their home. In Texas, it was a subtle way to let people know how much money you spent on your home, apparently a way to impress others or to humble oneself ... weird. Anyway, we had a wonderful long weekend together.

Christmas was uneventful. Sales were down at the Harley dealership, and you could tell the market was continuing to turn to shit. Interest rates were rising, and the Motor Company continued to ship motorcycles despite the dealers' cry of "No more bikes!" The only thing that Christmas was marked by was the sad fact that my mother was dying. It was on Christmas Day that she could no longer muster up the energy to visit anyone in the family for the holiday celebration. I flew down to see Dana for New Year's Eve, and she finally told a friend about me so that she could have a babysitter for our New Year's celebration. We had a wonderful night planning the future, talking about our life together, and figuring out exactly how we would do that … once again with excellent champagne and a wonderful dinner. We stared into each other's eyes and made each other promises of our commitment. We brought in the New Year making love in every room of her new apartment.

Late that January, my mother died. She died of cancer but never complained. My brothers and sisters and I took care of her for the last two weeks of her life. We did have hospice help us every evening and then twenty-four hours a day near the end. We all cried like we were children. I tried to drink the pain away, but every morning it looked at me in the mirror and would not turn away. So I drank more and more. I really started to slide downhill. My mother was nearly ninety years old, and as you can imagine all the memories of my childhood came flooding into my mind. I couldn't stop thinking, but my mind was numb. I wondered why I felt so sad. I loved my mother, I'd visited her often, and we had as much in common as a son can have with his mother. Boys are always closer to their father and girls are just closer to their mother … I guess that's just the way it is. So why did I feel so low when I had my girl only a phone call away? Well, maybe I should say only a quick airline flight away. Perhaps it was many things: business was bad, the Motor Company didn't seem to care, it was the dead of winter, and I had lost one of the strongest women I had ever known, my mom. Maybe if I share with you a paper I wrote in college about my mom, it will help you understand who I had lost.

This was a paper for my first college class in written communication. The title of the paper is, "Harley Men Love Their Mothers, Too":

As I sat on the kitchen floor, my legs stretched out in front of me, the small powder blue record player, with its abused needle, scratched out a song "Daaaaaveeeey, Daaaveeey Crocket, King of the wild frontier ... kilt him a bear when he was only three ..." At five years old my legs weren't very long but they still protected "my" record player. It was mine every day until my older brothers and sisters would come home from school.

A warm cuddly contentment surrounded me as my mother stood at the sink and washed the lunch dishes. Her white and blue apron had its strings tied just so. I loved it when my mom came home from work. She made me feel like I was the only little boy in the whole world!

Waking me from my musical trance, she would say, "Okay, speedy Gonzalez, let's go take a nap." And with the quickness of that speedy little mouse, I would race down the hallway, turn into my bedroom, and be ready in bed before she got there. These were just some of my childhood memories. Memories of a very special mother. But let me explain just what a unique person she is.

Mary Theodor was born in the heart of Milwaukee in 1920. Adversity faced her nearly all of her childhood and adolescence. By 1929 the Depression had affected everyone who wasn't rich. Her family wasn't rich. As a disastrous blow not only to the family, but especially to a nine-year-old girl, her father died as a result of an accident. The truck he was unloading backed up and crushed his chest against the loading dock. Her comprehension of death was only to try to understand that daddy was never coming home again. She spent countless nights crying herself to sleep.

Her mother raised four daughters and one son alone. It was bad enough being poor; it was nearly unbearable to be on county welfare. There was never enough money for anything. My mom worked any job she could to help, mainly housecleaning. As she got older, she would scrub floors to save money for college.

With her excellent grades in high school, she was accepted into nursing school. Milwaukee County General Hospital had one of the toughest nursing programs in the Midwest. She labored her way through the nursing school curriculum and graduated in 1942, second in her class! Only six months after graduation she married my father.

My father Ed was an ambitious entrepreneur starting in the printing business after his tour in the U.S. Navy in Okinawa during World War II. My mother began work immediately as a nurse. Through the next several decades my mom worked full-time and raised seven children. As you can imagine, seven kids can brew up a lot of trouble for their parents. She had to deal with everything from rebel boys, runaways, teen pregnancy, and cults to broken bones and broken hearts. She can cook, sew, knit, crochet, needlepoint, oil paint, and complete a crossword puzzle faster than anyone I've ever known. Her garden of roses and other beautiful flowers is the envy of everyone who sees it. But most of all, she cares for each one of her children as an individual. Just like she did for me, always making each one of us feel uniquely special. An old Moroccan proverb states, "In the eyes of its mother, every beetle is a gazelle." To this day she will do anything for me or my brothers and sisters. She only asks what many mothers ask, "Why don't you call more often?"

I say my mother is unique because I know of no other woman who has overcome such dramatic childhood adversity, the Great Depression and poverty, worked her way through college, then worked full-time and raised seven children. She has my awe and admiration. Sometimes she slips my mind, but every now and again something will happen or someone will say something like what happened at work a while ago that will make me remember this special relationship.

A young woman coworker at Harley-Davidson by the name of Denise said to me, "It's very nice working with you. You must have a very wonderful mother." All I could say through the lump in my throat was, "Yes ... yes I do."

The end.

It was an interesting end of winter and beginning of spring with this new girl. I flew down to Texas two to three times per month. I got to learn a lot more about her marriage. From her description, the guy was a mama's boy and also a hillbilly. He was a drug addict and even stole money from her. And of course he was the kind of guy who didn't even stay at the hospital after she had her baby. He went out to party and snort cocaine. After about a year or so, according to her, she found out he was having an affair with some woman for about a year. She could never get the total truth out of him, but she tape-recorded him without his knowledge and busted them. It seemed like a typical divorce process except that he would cry like a sissy and even told her mother that he had his guns and would kill anyone who was with her. Ooooh … I was shaking in my boots! Right!

Dana and I planned our work ahead of us and worked our plan. We figured out how I would integrate into her son's life, her friends' lives, and her coworkers' lives. She seemed most concerned about her boss at the dealership and what he would think about me. It took her about one year to tell her family and friends about me. She wouldn't tell them until her divorce was final, even though her estranged husband was living with another girl. I don't know what this guy had over her, but he sure could make her upset. I can't tell you how many times a thirty-second phone call would turn her into a crying fool. I felt so bad for her. Hard to deal with the fact that someone she was trying to remove from her life had more control over her emotions than I did. At least that's the way it seemed to me. When the divorce was final, she changed her name back to her maiden name. I was hoping it was for me, but she did it because it was less expensive to legally change her name back at the end of the divorce. Go figure.

The next year was one of the most wonderful years of my life. My partner, Chaz, and I were working on his takeover of the dealership. We were working our plan of him taking over each department one after another. I had tremendous respect for his goal-orientation, but I was very concerned with his Human Resource skills.

No one seemed to like him. Some of my best employees wanted to leave. But I had made a commitment to him and to myself and to his family, and I don't go back on my commitments. Sales, at the dealership and nationwide, continued to trend downward, and the Motor Company continued to jam motorcycles down our throats with rising interest rates and floor-plan charges growing at a geometric rate. We had been banking with Samson Bank. They had promised us the world. Everyone at the bank liked the sex appeal of the Harley dealership. They loved how Chaz and I were managing the decimal dust of the financial statement. In one simple meeting with the president—Patty, what a girlie name—and the vice president, I was asked if I had any funny stories. I vaguely described the laundry-room scene from the cruise, and apparently it delighted the vice president but offended the president of the bank. Apparently, he was an anti-male. After promising Milwaukee Harley-Davidson that they would renew all loans and lines of credit, they called our loan due. We had no alternative but to find another banking source, and *fast!* To this day, Samson Bank can suck my ass. They are two-faced liars and cheats. Their commercials claim they are family company, and that's exactly what they told us—that we would be treated like family. That was bullshit. Even their commercials talk about being a "family company." Right. The Samson family gets rich at the expense of others. Chaz worked very diligently on securing financing. We were also in arrears with Harley-Davidson Motor Company. We were honest with them, they knew our situation, and we met with them at least on a monthly basis and kept our promises. If we could not fulfill any of our obligations, we would contact them immediately. This seemed to work. But the pressure was becoming unbearable. Sales kept going down, expenses kept creeping up, and the Motor Company had no idea how to help us, no matter how much we begged. At the time, it was obvious that they had amateurs running these major departments. Our future was in inept hands. I started to pray, and pray very hard.

On one of my trips down to Texas, I got to meet Dana's family. I knew I was in love. She had a fantastic family. They were so much like mine—big family events often, with everyone bringing food and having a good time. Everyone helping clean up, tons of kids running around, and just an all-around great family atmosphere. I thought I'd fit right in … at least, that's the way it felt. One night I asked her why her parents had gotten divorced, and she reluctantly said that her mother had an affair with a teenager from their neighborhood. Apparently, the affair lasted for quite a while—with a teenager! I can tell you this, I was stunned. She said that she was not very proud of her mother and what the woman had done and how badly it had hurt her father. It bothered her so much that when her parents got divorced, she lived with her father and not her mother. That's probably where she learned to not care about long-term relationships. I mean, I agree that infidelity is a dead-end to any marriage. But I can't imagine being a young girl, of teenage years, finding out your mother is having sex with some kid who hangs out at your house from the neighborhood! As time went on, she began to introduce me to more and more of her friends and coworkers. In a triumphant move, she decided it was time to tell her boss about me. Up until this point, no one really knew that she had met me while she was still married and had been having an affair with me on her husband. In fact, her mother thought I was married and that I was having an affair. Ha-ha, isn't that funny! Well, unexpectedly, her boss's response to learning about me was that he was jealous. Kind of an odd statement/response. Of course, my girlfriend and I were soon to find out that her boss was dating a nineteen-year-old girl who worked at the dealership as a cleaning lady. Dana would later refer to him as an odd guy. She was always creeped out about that. But what could she do? I didn't see anything wrong with the age difference between her boss and his girlfriend, because they seemed so compatible. In time I would become good friends with both of them.

The time had come for me to meet her son. I had never had children except in high school. When I met her son, I had someone else to fall in love with, and I fell in love with her son big-time—even though the first words out of his mouth when we met were, "I hate you!" Oh, what kids will do to endear themselves to you. Those were the only unkind words ever spoken between us. We grew to love each other as a family. He finally had a stable male figure in his life. I taught him to say prayers, and the first time he saw his mom and I kiss was at the zoo when he was going to take our picture and he asked me to kiss her and I did so on the cheek. That wasn't good enough for him; he wanted me to kiss her like a boyfriend would kiss his girlfriend. Her father made a deal with her that if she would evict an old friend of his from a rental property, she could have the house. She had the guts to do it, and she did it. Her father's old friend was a piece of work. Drug user, con artist, fat slob, and idiot. The house was a pigsty. She slowly cleaned the garbage and furniture out of the house and got everything put into her name. I began fixing, painting, and getting the house ready to move in. I painted every single room, fixed every appliance, did all the landscaping, and helped her move from the apartment to her new house. It was a nice small house, after I fixed it up, in a lower-middle-class neighborhood. But the neighborhood had a pool, and that meant when I wasn't working on the house I could swim and sunbathe. I didn't move in any of my furniture but continued to travel back and forth from Milwaukee to Texas. The days rolled by; every trip to Milwaukee was stressful, and the Motor Company was bearing down hard. She and I would go out dancing, and I taught her to dance to music other than rap. I hate rap music! Did you know that the letter *C* is silent in word *rap*? We also began to have arguments. We mainly argued about her ex-husband and the constant contact that they had, as they argued every time they communicated. I was getting very frustrated … and began to drink more. She would also change plans at a moment's notice and forget to tell me. She would make plans and then change them on me. I would try to talk to her about this, but it always turned into an argument because she could never be wrong. Her response, many times, would be, "That's the way I roll." She started working more and more hours, even more than the six days a week she was already working.

It was the night before Father's Day, and I was leaving for Milwaukee to celebrate with my family. Some of the neighborhood guys had come over, unexpectedly, with their own beer in coolers. As the night wore on, I thought it was prudent that she and I go to bed and make love, as I wouldn't see her for about a week. When I told the guys that it was getting late and I had to get up early, they apologized and left. As soon as the door closed, she flipped her shit! She started screaming that I wasn't her father and I had no right to kick people out of her house. It was her house, and I should just leave and go to Milwaukee. She was drunk. She grabbed her car keys, and despite my pleading, she got in her car and drove to her mother's house. By the way, her mother lived about an hour away. That was the first big red flag. No one tells this woman what to do, and she does no wrong. A lesson I should have learned then and there.

We got over that and promised each other that we would talk these issues out instead of her kicking me out or running away. She never could keep a promise. From that point on, any time she was angry at me she would do one of two things: kick me out and tell me to go to Milwaukee or attempt to deny me some type of privilege having to do with her son. Maybe because she knew, because I said so many times, that he meant the world to me.

The week before school started for her son, she went to a parent-teacher greeting. She saw that approximately 30 percent of his class was going to be Hispanic. Neither of us was prejudiced, but we realized that these children needed interpreters because they spoke very little English. We could also conclude that this would take away, even if just a little, from her son's education. So we decided to look at moving. I ended up buying a piece of property that was closer to her family and in an outstanding neighborhood, a gated community, as well as one of the best school districts in the area. The house plans that she and I decided on—or should I say, she decided on—were purchased, and I hired a contractor. I started by having septic and water put in the property. As this was all happening, she went out on her own while I was out of town and looked at another house and decided to buy that house. Even though I did love the home she chose, I was a little miffed that I had bought this land and paid for the plans (and architectural changes made per her request) only to have her change her mind before even discussing it with me. Fortunately, I only lost a few thousand dollars on that deal, as I was able to sell the property very quickly. It was at this time that we decided I should move down to Texas. My girlfriend and her mother went shopping and picked the furniture that they wanted me to move to her new house. At the same time, I was making arrangements for Chaz to buy me out according to our agreement. Chaz looked and looked and looked for partners and found nothing. However, we came up with a deal that would fulfill my meager needs, and we signed that deal with his promise to make sure I was taken care of (as he was my retirement). He was so grateful for the opportunity to get into the dealership. Oh, how quickly he forgot those promises.

I put my house up for sale, and I moved my furniture and started fixing up and buying things for our new house. I mean, for *her* house. I'd been waiting a long time for this to happen. I went to my jeweler in Milwaukee and bought a ring and asked her to marry me on October 31, which was our two-year anniversary. I wanted her to marry me, and I felt that I should not live in the house with her son without at least being engaged. We had so much fun at the new house. We also had so much fun building our family. We went on many trips including New York City, Disneyland, the Texas coast beaches, the Bahamas, Europe, and back and forth to Milwaukee many times. My family also fell in love with her and her son. I thought it was a match made in heaven. I could even put up with the constant complaints when she would come home from work accusing her assistant of being fat and lazy or that some of the cashiers were thieves. She would complain about her sister, who was recovering from drug addiction (crystal meth), and about her brother-in-law, who everybody hated. He seemed to be a compulsive liar, but I always liked the guy. He always seemed like he was full of crap, but he proved to me that he could back up whatever he bragged about.

I think one of the toughest times for me was when she was lying on my lap and started to cry because her ex-husband had gotten in a motorcycle accident (not serious) and her boss's son had gotten in a car accident. She cried for half an hour about how horrible her life would be if she lost either one of them. Made *me* feel real good! I was starting to see that this was her world, and I was only a small part of it. Even though I took care of the house, did all the grocery shopping, paid for all of our trips, did all the cooking, and paid every bill except for the mortgage, I could see that this was *her* house and *her* life. And then she kicked me out again over some stupid fight—probably dealing with her not communicating with me, which was very typical, because she felt too much communication from me, or to me, was controlling, and she couldn't be free. On that particular incident, I called her from Milwaukee and asked if she was serious about dismantling our family. She said no, that she was sorry and she wanted help, and I should help her find someone who could help us. It was at about this time that my dog, my faithful companion and friend of seventeen years, died. Again, I was heartbroken. She was the best dog I or any one of my friends ever knew. I drank the pain away.

Dana had decided that the ring I bought for her engagement was not her style. I was fine with that, because I didn't really like it if she didn't like it. She began to look at different rings and decided on a custom designer setting made in New York, with a nearly two-carat diamond. It was absolutely stunning. The diamond was nearly flawless, and you could see it from across a large room. She wore it so proudly once we finally got it. That's a story in itself. The ring had to be resized and was to be shipped to me a couple days before Christmas. I tracked it, I called the manufacturer, I called the jeweler, and we couldn't find it! I was pissed off. Her family Christmas party came and went, and on Christmas afternoon the doorbell rings. It was FedEx; they had forgot to deliver it the day before, so it turned out to be another Christmas present for her. You know, I look back at it now and I think of all the things, some little, some big, that I did to build that relationship, and I wonder why? I mean, I know why, I was in love with her, I was in love with her son, I was in love with her family, I was in love with her friends, and I was in love with her coworkers. I bought her fresh flowers every week. I sent her hundreds of romantic cards, texts, and e-mails.

The relationship got better for about a year, and then things really started to change. It was small things at first, such as she would get perturbed if I sent her any type of text message. She would call me at the last minute and ask me to pick up her son from his after-school activities. If I explained that I was in the middle of cooking, she would get upset and say, "Fine! I'll pick him up myself." She started asking me to do all of her "running around" chores. Return this, return that, go to the store. Make arrangements for this or that. Call this person or make an appointment to do something.

The lovemaking became less and less, and farther in between. I kept trying to figure it out as well as ask her what was going on. What had changed? What was the matter? Not so long ago, she couldn't keep her hands off of me. We did all the things normal couples do. We made it a point to make love in every room of the new house. She took pictures of us making love and doing some kinky things. She bought some sex toys for us to use in our lovemaking. Some things were the same, such as the girl could never give a good blow job. And she hated to give hand jobs and would even refuse to do it. That was frustrating, for a man needs some attention. What was weird was that she loved to perform anal kissing on me. She would lick my behind for five minutes. And she always wanted me to perform oral sex on her before we had sexual intercourse. If we hadn't made love in a long time, I would tease her and tell her that I was going to masturbate. She'd always thought that was funny until now, when she started claiming that it really hurt her feelings. The sex was good when we had it, but once or twice a month was not cutting it for me. I finally understood why her ex-husband had an affair. She was so selfish and concerned about herself and her happiness that she didn't care about anybody else.

Even when she came home from work, as time progressed, her attitude was starting to change to more of a hostile and irritated demeanor. She would tell me how stupid the people were at work. There was one girl, a newlywed, who busted her new husband surfing porn on the Internet and even looking up dating websites. Danaold me how stupid this girl was for even considering marrying this guy. She was almost becoming passive-aggressive. She would bitch about her girlfriends. She had one friend she'd never really liked. She had this friend paint several rooms in the house and constantly complained to me that it wasn't what she expected and that she was being overcharged. She had friends who were very Christian, and she kept telling me how weird they were for using their children in antiabortion protests. I mean, I couldn't get her to stop complaining to me about anything and everything. I could tell she was frustrated at work. She was overworked and underpaid, and did an outstanding job. She knew she was underpaid and I agree that she was. She should have been making twice as much money. And I think in a big way, her boss was always taking advantage of her. I mean, he gave her a used watch for her ten-year anniversary. Sure, it was a Rolex, but it was used! She liked the watch, but a cash bonus would've gotten a lot more mileage. He always was penny wise and dollar foolish.

I started drinking before she ever got home just to

take the edge off. I even started hiding vodka in the trunk of my car. She continued to drink about the same, which wasn't often, but she started buying weed. And I don't mean just a little bit—she bought it by the bagful. Something was going wrong; she wouldn't talk about it, never had a discussion on a meaningful level because she "hated confrontation." For someone as communicative and articulate as I am, that was maddening. I began losing weight; I felt more and more depressed, and my anxiety level was increasing dramatically. I started to see my personal physician looking for answers and praying to God for help. I knew Dana didn't want me to drink as much, and I really wanted to reduce my level of intake. All the while, during the early part of that winter, Chaz kept calling me and telling me how bad things were at the dealership. He would almost cry on the telephone and tell me that we were running out of money and needed to refinance but he couldn't find a bank to help him. All this as Christmas 2009 approached. January 1 would be the deadline for the bank to pull our line of credit and call our loan note due. Stress, stress, stress!

Despite the impending doom and the failing relationship, we had a great Christmas, and she and her son came to Milwaukee with me to celebrate New Year's Eve with my family and friends. It was great. We had fresh snow, and her son loved playing outside and even doing shoveling. I guess you can only find that funny if you lived in the northern states where every kid hated the very thought of having to shovel snow. Over the next few weeks, our life remained status quo. I did, however, have to make the most excruciating decision in my business life.

My partner informed me that we either had to file for bankruptcy or find a new bank. Many hours of discussion ensued. We both got our separate attorneys involved, and it appeared that the only solution was for me to take it in the shorts. It was either get "some" money (ten cents on the dollar) or nothing at all. Well, my partner and friend had promised to take care of me, and we did end up settling for pennies on the dollar. I got fucked in the ass. To this day, he has not gone out of his way to help me at all. You know what they say—with friends like that, who needs enemies? Chaz and I signed the final paperwork on the last day of January 2010.

Two months later, on Valentine's Day, I could see the writing on the wall with my fiancée. Her son and I (well, I) got her gifts of jewelry and several Valentine's Day love cards. I got a small box of six chocolates. I just knew it was the end. We didn't even make love that night. Two days later, we got in a very small argument in which, after I had cooked a well-planned-out dinner, she wanted me to cook her son something different, without a logical explanation. I got so angry that I just had to leave the house. I was planning on going to Milwaukee for the weekend anyway, but halfway to the airport I realized that it was stupid to leave now, and I turned around and went back home (I should say to her home). The next day, I went to my doctor and explained my irrational behavior, and he suggested that I start taking Lexapro. I discussed that with my fiancée when she got home from work, and her response was to say, "Oh great, you are an addict!"

I decided it was time to give her some space, and I left for Milwaukee the next day planning on staying for the weekend.

I received a text message the next day after my arrival in Milwaukee. It was a message in response to my message telling her that I hoped she was having a great day and that I loved her. Her response via text was, "Bob, I love you too, but I'm done working on this relationship. It's over!"

CHAPTER 24

IN REHAB . . . OVER AND OUT!

EVERY NOISE WHEN YOU are in a hospital seems amplified times ten. Throughout the night and especially in the early hours of the morning, when you are trying to sleep, why is it that the nurses insist on waking you up to check your blood pressure, temperature, and other vitals? I was so exhausted that all I wanted to do was sleep and sleep and sleep. I wanted to sleep for as long as I could. And as if the constant interruptions by the medical staff weren't enough, there was a mystery woman wearing high heels who kept walking the halls of the hospital near my room. Her footsteps echoed like the sound of the German army doing the goosestep in a military parade. From my Valium-induced haze, I swear she walked up and down those halls five times a night every night that I was ther' I later found out from the hospital staff that the wom' making the rounds was in charge of the drug and al' rehab program, which I was about to begin. S' continuously checking for her next victim, wh' be completing inpatient detox. As soon as the ' released by the doctor, she would personally escort that individual down to the classroom so that there was no possibility of escape.

Ever since I came back from Texas, I had been suffering a deep depression. The daily anxiety attacks had grown to an unbearable level. I mean, look at my situation. I had just been screwed out of 90 percent or more of my price for the sale of Milwaukee Harley-Davidson. I would soon lose my health benefits—all because, in my opinion, we had somehow nearly driven the dealership into bankruptcy. I really was convinced that this was Chaz's plan from the beginning, and he was being coached by our old business acquaintance, the guy who helped me finance the buyout. This guy had told me several times that he had used this tactic in taking over businesses he had been part of many years ago. Basically, he waited until the business could no longer support the debt structure to the prior owner, and then he offered the choice of bankruptcy or pennies on the dollar. I had just broken up with my fiancée and lost any contact with her son. I was kicked out of her house; I had no clothes, no computer, and only slow access to my bank accounts. My car was stuck at the airport in Texas, and she was demanding that I move my belongings out of her house immediately. The only thing that seemed to numb the pain was drinking, and man oh and man, did I drink!

My brother Jimmy had been doing some work at my other house in Milwaukee, it was a hundred-year-old rental house that I had been restoring for almost twenty years. I moved into that house. He had been sober for bout seven years, and he continued to talk to me about how much I was drinking. Every day he would come over, and every day we would have the same conversation. He would ask how much I had been drinking, and I would reply "more and more." He started to tell me stories about his drinking days, of which I was a part of until he got married. When we were younger, we hung out and drank together, but after he married that all changed. Probably for the better. Well, he talked to me about how damaging drinking had been to his marriage, his personal life, and his professional life. I really didn't listen; I just heard the words. I kept drinking, heavily.

In the meantime, Dana kept calling and demanding that I make arrangements to move out of her house. By this point, I was so paralyzed by my own self-pity, guilt, self-loathing, and alcoholism that I couldn't move, and I mean that literally. My brother came over one morning, early, and asked me if we were going down to Texas and on which day we would be going. At this point, I couldn't think anymore, and I broke down. I cried uncontrollably for half an hour. He tried to console me but to no avail. Between my sobs, I told him that I needed to quit drinking, that I needed help, and that I could not do it by myself. I asked if he would call our sister, who worked at a large local hospital as the director of medical staff services. My sister Gini and her husband, Billy, were at my house within thirty minutes. Once again, between the tears, I explained that I needed help, as I could not face anything in my life any longer. This was on Saturday, March 13, 2010. Gini called some of her friends at the hospital and made arrangements for me to be admitted into the inpatient/outpatient program for drug and alcohol abuse on Monday morning, March 15. I immediately felt one of the boulders being lifted off my shoulders. I spent the rest of the day drinking up what remaining booze I had in the house, and Billy picked me up at 7:30 the next morning. After a lengthy and nerve-racking admissions process, I was admitted into detox.

The next six months were some of the most difficult months of my life. My dad and best friend had health issues that were worsening at a geometric rate. He was suffering from a failing heart and respiratory disease. After two heart bypass surgeries and at the age of ninety, he was dying—a reality that no son or daughter wants to face. I also had to continue to try to make plans to move my furniture from Texas back to my house in Milwaukee. Although Dana tried to be nice, it was easy to see through her façade; she was long over the relationship and was making a curiously urgent effort to move on with her life. She was not making it easy to communicate with her, and I found out that she was already seeing someone who initiated contact with her (from her past) through Facebook and in person. My ex-partner, Chaz, was not able to pay me the money he owed on another business venture. I felt that he was actually just showing his true colors to me, finally.

After being released from the hospital, I attended rehab sessions three days a week. I wanted to drink every single minute, but I never had a drop of alcohol. Being addicted to drugs or alcohol, I once heard, is like being out in the ocean, and even though you have a life jacket on, the huge swells and waves just keep pushing you in any direction they want any time they want. It is a very helpless feeling of not being in control and of not having self-control. It comes from deep inside your being and is as much a part of you as all of your memories combined. Some say that it is a disease. I can see that. I needed the stability in life brought on by a higher power. I decided I needed more help and started going to AA meetings and following the twelve steps in their program and renewing my belief and faith in God. It started to work. I felt this way: Picture Michelangelo's painting of man reaching out toward God. Now picture the worst image you have of the devil. Now picture me, reaching toward God, and my index-finger nail is hanging on to his index-finger nail. On the other end is the devil holding on to a chain that is connected to an iron forged shackle around my ankle. I felt like that every day!

In addition to going to weekly meetings with my outpatient group and attending church religiously, I started seeing a therapist who specialized in addiction. In our first session, she asked me what I wanted to achieve by seeing her. In my heart and soul, I knew the answer: I would not leave until I figured out the reasons behind the deep anxiety that always plagued me and sent me to the bottle. Wow, I am so glad I did that. For the next six months, through classes, AA, church, and one-on-one counseling, I discovered several axioms that are now at the forefront in guiding my own life. First, I needed to love God more than anyone else. Second, and very important, I needed to not allow myself to create drama in my life or let anyone else create drama in my life. And last, but of no less importance, I would always need some type of group, like AA, as continued support to maintain my sobriety.

I came home from my last therapy session and saw an e-mail message from my brother David stating that he had visited our father that day and Dad was unable to get out of bed. The message had not much more information than that. So I decided I'd better get over to my dad's and see if he needed help. I was there for the next three months. If you haven't read *Tuesdays with Morrie* or haven't had a parent who took a long time to pass away and was involved in hospice, you might not understand the rest of this. When people get involved with the end-of-life of another person, whether they know it or not, they're about to get involved in the most life-changing event for both of them. I think it was a Thursday by the time I got to my dad's house, and he was actually in better spirits. He was sitting on the couch with the oxygen tubes in his nose eating cereal. He greeted me, in a weakened voice, with the familiar, "Hey there, Bowzer!"

For the next several months, week after week, day after day, I watched my father slowly deteriorate until he was a shell of the man I had known my entire life. During that period of time, we talked even more than we had our entire close life together. He talked openly about my mom and stepmom and his love for both of them. . He talked about his love for his children, probably more than anything else. You know, people talk about how the elderly have no holds barred when they speak about their past, and my father did not hesitate to talk about some things that we normally would think of as off-limits. As an example, my father would constantly tell anyone within earshot, including my brothers and sisters, that I was his best friend in the world. It was embarrassing. I completely understood, but it was embarrassing nonetheless. One thing I could never get him to talk about in detail was his time in World War II. He was receiving compensation for an injury he received during his service in Okinawa. He was a medical aide, and I am sure that the sights he saw were devastating. The few things that he did say were mainly about how the bombs, grenades, and mortar shells pounded their camp all day and night. Apparently he suffered tremendous headaches from the concussion of the explosions coupled with taking care of his fellow soldiers who were maimed by the attacks.

I had been attending a church several blocks from my home—Fox Point Lutheran Church—every Sunday since I came back from Texas. I convinced my father that he would love it and that it was far better than the church he was attending and had been for years. During that period of time, as he continued to decline in health and finally ended up in a wheelchair, I was amazed at how many church members would comment after the service on how endearing it was to watch how I took care of my father. Every morning and every night, I would read him passages from the Bible. Oh, how he loved that. Even during the middle of the day, when we had a boring moment, I would ask him if he wanted me to read him some of the Bible, and he would perk up and say yes. Cramming for exams!

I met a woman from England online through my cousin-in-law via Facebook. We chatted a lot during my father's final three months, and it was a great comfort. She was estranged from her husband, and we planned to meet as soon as possible. I went to England two times and shagged her rotten, only to find out she was ensconced in her marriage and there was no future for us, at least a foreseeable future. Once again, one dagger in the back and one in the heart.

As the time Dad and I were spending together was during the deepest part of our Wisconsin winter, I tried to keep the TV on the Golf Channel. Not only did Dad love that, but we had that as well as many other things in common. My father was, and is, the golf champion at Lincoln Park Golf Course in Milwaukee, Wisconsin. He had the lowest score ever shot on that course. He and I probably played that course a thousand times, and I think that every time we played it he reminded me that at one time the course was an eighteen-hole full course that extended to the other side of the Milwaukee River. Every moment in that golf cart with him was something very special. When I was still with Milwaukee Harley, I recall that nearly every time we played, I would get a call on my cell phone from either Harley corporate, Paul Kegel, or Chaz, and he never complained. He would only ask, with great concern, "Is everything okay, Bowzer?" My dad was so staunch about the rules of golf, yet he let me answer my phone as needed while we played. I could feel his heartstrings pull when the phone call was bad and I had to let off steam. The last time we golfed was in mid-November with his personal physician, Mike, and his cardiologist, Brian. We were only able to play five holes because it was about fifty degrees and a little bit misty, with a wind that chilled you to the bone. (We didn't finish, but we did however play the next day, which was much warmer.)

The last few days that my father was alive, he insisted on having meetings with his primary physician, Mike, and his cardiologist, Brian, as well as the nurse from hospice. He discussed his options and his determination about his willingness to accept his end-of-life. These meetings were extremely difficult and emotional for me, and thank God, at most of them, I had my brothers Tommy, Eddie, Jimmy, David and/or my sisters Gini or Oody present to share the burden of my father's requests. After he had announced his wishes for passing, it was only a matter of a day or two before I began administering morphine for his agitation and discomfort. I remember calling my sister one morning after giving him a dose of morphine and telling her that he seemed like a bionic machine. I could not calm him down, and it seemed like he had the energy of a teenager. I was confused, frustrated, and scared. It took about three hours for the morphine to take effect. Late that evening, with his head in my lap, he briefly woke up and reached up, and while rubbing my arm, all he could say was, "Thank you, thank you, thank you, thank you!"

My father enriched every life he touched. He did that by treating people as equals, human beings, to be respected and loved as God teaches. Everyone at the MIT class I took understood you have to treat people like human beings. You really do have to love people and not look at them as subordinates, workers, employees, or anything less than you. Once an organization has adopted any position contrary to that concept—as an HR tool—I think it is doomed to failure. The current Harley-Davidson infrastructure has embraced a concept that the product means nothing and that the stock market dictates what they should and should not do. God will help those of us who fought for Harley-Davidson with everything we had, sacrificing our personal lives, and are horrified by what is currently happening in the corporation.

I put my dad to bed and set my alarm for three a.m. I thought that I would get up in the middle of the night and check on him to make sure he was doing okay. I'm so glad I did, because when I got up and went to check on him, he was lying on his back and his mouth was filled with black fluid from his lungs. He was still breathing with great difficulty through his nose. I gently rolled him over and cleared out his throat and cleaned him up. I went back to bed, setting my alarm for seven a.m. The date was March 27—my deceased mother's birthday. I'd arranged for my sister and her husband to take care of my dad during the morning so that I could attend church. My dad had slipped into a comatose state, but he seemed to be comfortable. The church service was wonderful as usual. However, I was quite emotional. After the service, I left the chapel and went into the community room to have my usual post-service cup of coffee and chat with some of the friends my father and I had made as members of the church. Something came over me, and I went back into the chapel to pray. I asked God for help in dealing with my current situation. I began to weep uncontrollably, and all of a sudden I heard a voice. It was the voice of God, and he said, "You and your father have paid a small price for him to come to meet me!" I instantly felt comfort and relief, and the satisfaction of knowing that everything would be all right. One of the pastors, Pastor Bruce, saw me in the chapel and came in to console me. I explained to them what happened and that I really was feeling good about everything. We said a prayer together and I left, heading back to my dad's place.

My dad passed away as I walked into the apartment. It was 12:35 p.m. He was surrounded by my brothers and sisters when he slipped away to meet the loved ones who had gone before him, and to meet his maker. I was actually feeling pretty good and was relieved that my father was no longer suffering in any way and was in eternal peace. The funeral was several days later. It was beautiful, a great service performed at our church by Pastor Dan. One of the beautiful young women from the church, Leila (she now performs with the Atlanta Ballet), sang "Shall We Gather by the River" and "Amazing Grace." My father had the military flag-presenting ceremony followed by taps. There wasn't a dry eye in the chapel. I didn't cry much and actually felt great about the funeral. My brothers and I were the pallbearers, and when we went to remove the casket I didn't realize that the funeral director was going to roll the casket out of the church on a gurney. So I was the only one of six trying to lift up and carry the entire weight of the casket. Needless to say, my back was out for three weeks afterward! The full weight of the emotions and stress and loss would not hit me until about six months later. The next six months, without doubt, proved to be the most difficult of my entire life. I must have reached for the phone to call my dad dozens of times after he was gone. Every time I wanted to play golf, every time I was watching golf on TV, the many times when I needed advice or support, or just the days when I had a few minutes and wanted to catch up, I had to stop myself, realizing that he was dead. I had lost not only my dad, but my best friend.

One of my friends, Carolyn from Harley, texted me that all the firsts would be the hardest. Like the first time I played golf without my dad, and my first Father's Day without my dad, and his first birthday without my dad. When the anniversary of his death and my mother's birthday came around, I pretty much lost it. I started drinking again. I fell down. I'm so sorry, Mom and Dad! I told anyone who cared that I had stumbled and fallen and got back up, brushed myself off, and carried on. My alcoholism no longer defined me; my struggle and journey would define me. I might stumble and fall, but I would never give up! On the threshold of success lie the bones of those who paused to rest and perished.

There is absolutely nothing better in the world to reset your mind than to take a long motorcycle ride, or many small short rides. And I did just that. I spent most of the rest of the year on my bike. I went to Europe twice and rode on dozens of short trips through the Kettle Moraine territory in south and central Wisconsin. It was only minutes from my home, so easy to get to and so incredibly beautiful. For those of you who really understand the sport of motorcycling, you know what I mean. For those of you who don't, I can't explain it. Because of my relationship with the Harley-Davidson Motor Company, I have seen the sunrise in Tokyo overlooking a Japanese garden with an old man performing tai chi. I have seen the sunset standing in a lake in Finland at one o'clock in the morning. I have visited nearly every continent on earth and met some of the most wonderful people in the world—Harley enthusiasts, employees, and dealers. Chaz and a few others are the exceptions to my meetings, friendships, and experiences.

You see where the stock is today, up and down based only on sales and profits. That's what it is all about now. You can see the sissy image in Harley's advertising. If you are a current customer, you can see how sissified the corporation has become. As of this writing, Willie G. Davidson has just retired.

Many years ago, when the demand for Harley-Davidsons far exceeded the supply, many companies started making their own version of the Harley-Davidson. I predicted at that time that the only company that even had a chance was Polaris, for several reasons. First of all, they were already producing an excellent product. They had the best snowmobiles and ATVs. Second, they had excellent manufacturing capabilities. Third, they had an exceptional grasp of the recreational market and the idiosyncrasies of that market. And fourth, they had a well-established and experienced distribution network, which included their dealers. As of this writing, Polaris has announced that they will be reintroducing the Indian motorcycle by 2013. If you are not familiar with the Indian motorcycle, it was the biggest competitor to Harley-Davidson as an American-made motorcycle. It was also extremely cool! It actually has a more nostalgic look than Harley-Davidson motorcycles. Mark my words, Polaris, with the newly Indian motorcycle, will give Harley-Davidson a run for its money.

Corporate greed ... hogs? Free enterprise and

capitalism must also embrace nurturing and the common and thoughtful humane treatment of employees. It is not just about money.

I believe we are here on this planet to look after those knocking from the outside and wanting to come in—those in need. Is laying off hundreds of employees and being more efficient an even trade for giving the top executives bonuses in excess of millions and millions? They can't spend that in a lifetime, yet they have ruined hundreds of employees' lives. Is that what it was all about? I never thought the Motor Company hogs would do that to the working man. The same person they made the machine for, to ride.

Is it time to sell your stock? Maybe, maybe not.

And as always, things end, not with a bang but with a whimper. Who is the real hog?

THE END

ABOUT THE AUTHOR

BOB MICHEL HAS BEEN in the motorcycle industry for twenty-nine years, fourteen of those with Harley-Davidson Motor Company He spent nine years as a partner and vice president of a franchised Milwaukee motorcycle dealership. Bob became sole owner of that dealership in July of 2003. As owner, he oversaw all the day-to-day operations, as he had since becoming involved with the dealership in 1996. Under his direction, dealership sales nearly tripled. He helped this American motorcycle company with almost all of its programs for its retail dealer network. His last position at the motorcycle company was manager of dealer facilities planning. Prior to that, Bob was manager of worldwide retail services. Earlier on, he held a variety of sales positions including district sales manager for Maryland, Virginia, Washington, DC, and part of North Carolina. He was part of the sales team that helped lead to the resurgence of this company. Bob has been treasurer of both local and state motorcycle associations. He is also co-author of the Executive Sales Academy Manual. He is a true motorcycle enthusiast who started riding when he was twelve years old and has owned more than twenty motorcycles. The story he has written is about his experience as an enthusiast, an employee of Harley Corporate, and a franchised Harley-Davidson dealer.